"John Calvin called the book of Psalms
us to pray these poems as our own prayer to God. They thus help us articulate our
heart to God, and they minister to us by drawing us close to him. Josh Moody does
a masterful job of leading us through the Psalms of Ascent in a way that touches
and transforms our lives."

**Tremper Longman III,** Robert H. Gundry Professor of Biblical Studies,
Westmont College

JOURNEY TO JOY

## Other Crossway books by Josh Moody

*Jonathan Edwards and Justification* (editor), 2012

*No Other Gospel: 31 Reasons from Galatians Why Justification by Faith Alone Is the Only Gospel*, 2011

# JOURNEY TO JOY

## The Psalms of Ascent

## JOSH MOODY

CROSSWAY

WHEATON, ILLINOIS

*Journey to Joy: The Psalms of Ascent*

Copyright © 2013 by Josh Moody

Published by Crossway
        1300 Crescent Street
        Wheaton, Illinois 60187

Cover design: Josh Dennis

Cover image: Salomon Lighthelm

First printing 2013

Printed in the United States of America

Unless otherwise indicated, Scripture quotations are from the ESV® Bible (*The Holy Bible, English Standard Version®*), copyright © 2001 by Crossway. 2011 Text Edition. Used by permission. All rights reserved.

Scripture quotations marked KJV are from the *King James Version* of the Bible.

All emphases in Scripture quotations have been added by the author.

Trade paperback ISBN: 978-1-4335-3497-3
PDF ISBN: 978-1-4335-3498-0
Mobipocket ISBN: 978-1-4335-3499-7
ePub ISBN: 978-1-4335-3500-0

**Library of Congress Cataloging-in-Publication Data**

Moody, Josh.
Journey to joy : the Psalms of ascent / Josh Moody.
    p. cm.
  Includes bibliographical references and index.
  ISBN 978-1-4335-3497-3
1. Bible. O.T. Psalms CXX–CXXXIV—Criticism, interpretation, etc.
I. Bible. O.T. Psalms CXX–CXXXIV. English. English Standard. 2013.
II. Title.
BS1445.S6M66      2013
223'.206—dc23                  2012028650

Crossway is a publishing ministry of Good News Publishers.

| VP | | 23 | 22 | 21 | 20 | 19 | 18 | 17 | 16 | 15 | 14 | 13 |
|----|----|----|----|----|----|----|----|----|----|----|----|----|
| 15 | 14 | 13 | 12 | 11 | 10 | 9 | 8 | 7 | 6 | 5 | 4 | 3 | 2 | 1 |

For Elianna—who daily teaches me more about Joy

# CONTENTS

# ACKNOWLEDGMENTS

First, let me offer a word of thanks to my executive assistants, who have skillfully helped me. I say "assistants" plural because this project was begun with the assistance of Pauline Epps, who then retired, and was completed with the assistance of Carolyn Litfin. I am indeed fortunate ("blessed," the Psalms would say rightly and more accurately, for they always insist on a theological vision) to have had the expert assistance of Pauline Epps and now the expert assistance of Carolyn Litfin.

I also wish to thank Crossway for agreeing to publish this project. Lane Dennis and all involved have, as always, excelled. Crossway is a remarkable ministry that is indeed God blessed and a blessing to me and to many, many other people. I thank God for you.

In addition, and in some ways most profoundly, I wish to thank the congregation of College Church. It is a joy to be on a journey together with a congregation that loves God's Word and the preaching of God's Word. I trust that this book, which many of you have asked to see published, will continue that journey to joy.

I also want to thank in particular the elders and pastors of College Church, who have a vision for God-centered, Word-driven ministry and with whom I am glad to serve.

As usual, and traditionally, though by no means perfunctorily, I wish to thank my family for their love and support. For Rochelle without whom my life would be far worse, for my children without whom my life would in addition be far more dull, and for the whole together without whom I would no doubt be yet more selfish than I probably still am. That Bilbo Baggins–like sentence in place, I need only say that I am so glad that God has given me you all. May we learn from the Psalms to combine truth with fire, logic with passion, and rhetoric with substance.

I also thank my parents. Many a time I remember seeing them read the Bible early in the morning, including the Psalms. For both ends of the spectrum of life, young and old, I trust this volume will encourage a journey back to the very center of God and so a renewed discovery of joy.

# PREFACE

Why the Psalms of Ascent? It is rare enough to study the Psalms, let alone this particular book within the book of Psalms. I suspect some will feel that the only reason to study a series of psalms like this is for antiquarian reasons, for purposes of academic interest, or at best to try to recapture a long-gone day when it was usual to sing psalms in church worship services. My reason for studying the Psalms, preaching them to our wonderful congregation at College Church, and now publishing them, is quite different.

I believe there is a crying need for people who believe the Bible to *feel* it. (And vice versa for those who *feel* Christianity, to know more about the Bible.) I know that, because in my own life I have experienced it. At one point in my life, though, I realized that while I knew God, and I knew he was true in an objective sense, subjectively my experience of God was significantly less than what I read about in the Bible. Where do you find in the Bible a solution to that malaise? David! The Psalms! There is a reason why Jesus frequently quotes from the Psalms and why the Psalms have proved a perennial favorite. They are *real*. They pull no punches. They tell it as it is. They scare people who wish the Bible said only things that sound pious and nice. But they also help you reconnect between the objective and the subjective, between the truth *about* God and the truth *of* God, between fear and faith, between failure and trust, between suffering and joy, and between hate and forgiveness. All the way through them is the theology of the cross, though the cross in a literal sense was unknown to the authors of the Psalms. And all the way through them is the theology of the resurrection, though Christ's resurrection in a literal sense was unknown to the original authors of the Psalms. They take your pain, and if you will, they transcend it by means of passion, the suffering of the soul in communion with God and his Messiah.

The Psalms are written to help us put our feelings in the right place. With all the ups and downs of life, we need to work those feelings through until we feel as we are meant to feel, and the Psalms give us what someone has called "Psalmnotherapy." You may know that some of the psalms say things that are quite honestly and bluntly horrible. But then quite honestly and bluntly, you and I feel things that are sometimes horrible. Because the psalms are *inspired* by God does not mean that every emotion in them is *approved* by God. In the Psalms you find people talking to God about their feelings openly in the context of the security of the covenant relationship between God and his people.

In particular, the Psalms of Ascent are a special collection of psalms put together in ancient Israel for this purpose. If you've looked at the Psalms of Ascent before, you will know that discovering that purpose is a little bit difficult because not every scholar agrees when they were written. We do not know what the ascent was that these psalms were *ascending*. Some scholars say that the psalms are ascending within their own poetic style, that there is a repeated refrain within them that ascends. One says "peace," so peace is repeated at the next poetic ascent; "deceit," and then deceit is repeated with the next step up in the poem, and so on. Several of these psalms do have this ascending pattern; it is particularly obvious in Psalm 130, but though these repetitions are in several of the Psalms of Ascent, not all of them have the same ascending poetic pattern. Indeed there are other psalms that also have this kind of ascending pattern. So the thought that this collection of psalms is called "Psalms of Ascent" because the poetry "ascends" does not quite explain their name.

Other scholars say that the Psalms of Ascent were sung at the return from Babylon, though those of us who think that the heading of the psalms (called the "ascription") is inspired and indicates direct authorship will not think that psalms said to be written by David could have been composed long after him. The Psalms of Ascent certainly could at least have been sung as God's people returned from Babylon, but apart from anything else, if the return from Babylon was the primary historical context, you would expect then that they would have been called Psalms of *an* Ascent rather than Psalms of Ascent.

The most common interpretation—and the one that I adopt for want of a better option—is that these psalms are pilgrim psalms, generally speaking. They are a journey from a long way away to the very heart of God, as represented by the three great pilgrim festivals in ancient Israel. We can imagine people singing these psalms as they went up to Jerusalem for a great festival. Even then, some of them seem more like something that you would write in your journal rather than sing with others, so perhaps they were also used to prepare the pilgrim privately or devotionally to make the great journey back to the very center of God.

Some also think that the fifteen psalms were used as the Levites moved up the fifteen steps from the Court of Women to the Court of Israel, perhaps in an increasingly higher tone, and again it is possible they were used that way. No doubt these psalms had different reference points and usages, as they do today. But whatever was the precise journey, they are intended to take us on a spiritual journey closer to God, through the various difficulties and trials that can come which might prevent that journey or derail us from it.

I rather like that term "psalmnotherapy." Some older people turn more and more to the Psalms, but not because the Psalms are only for old people. It's like poetry. The golden age of poetry is either youthful adolescent woes or aged whimsy or whenever there is a need for emotional turmoil to be expressed. Unlike our poetry, the Psalms are a God-designed tool to help us feel truly the truth. Psalms say things we would rarely say out loud in church. But, then, people feel things they would rarely say out loud in church. We need somewhere to go to process those emotions, to inspect them in the light of God, and bring them into line with his will and his way.

Such is the great gift of all the psalms, and the Psalms of Ascent, in particular, are a coherent path along which we may travel to the center of God. Whatever their precise historical origin, and no one knows for sure, though everyone has a theory, they are intended to help us make a pilgrimage back to God. We might start far away, even in a land of gossip and slander, but gradually, by following their path, we can end up in a place where there is "blessing."

That does not mean you have to have some problem that needs fixing to enjoy the Psalms of Ascent. As Bunyan realized, we are all on a journey, or pilgrimage, as Christians, and these psalms are a perfect companion to a modern *Pilgrim's Progress*, or to an adventure novel of traveling fiction with a motif of journey at its heart, like *Lord of the Rings*.

When you read the Psalms of Ascent, you should think of yourself as embarking. You are starting a journey.

It is *your* journey. It is all in relation to God, centers on God, and is intended to honor God. But the psalms frequently (and shockingly for some theologians) love to use the first-person pronoun *I, me,* or *my,* as well as the corporate language of plural *we.* It is rarely *them* or *they* who are addressed or described, though that of course is there often enough, but it is not the driving feeling of the psalms. As my "journey to joy" starts and carries on, I find that I am lost in wonder, love, and praise in God, and so I become increasingly God centered and gospel centered.

That's my prayer. Enjoy these psalms. They are meant to be read, sung, digested, wrestled over, and most of all put in your backpack and taken with you on a spiritual journey to the father heart of God.

A SONG OF ASCENTS.
In my distress I called to the LORD,
 and he answered me.
Deliver me, O LORD,
 from lying lips,
 from a deceitful tongue.
What shall be given to you,
 and what more shall be done to you,
 you deceitful tongue?
A warrior's sharp arrows,
 with glowing coals of the broom tree!
Woe to me, that I sojourn in Meshech,
 that I dwell among the tents of Kedar!
Too long have I had my dwelling
 among those who hate peace.
I am for peace,
 but when I speak, they are for war!
—Psalm 120

# 1

# PEACE

If someone has lied about you, perhaps someone you trusted, you know how much it hurts. Of course people say nasty things all the time. Children can be especially cruel with their words. In fact, I sometimes wonder whether many of the apparently sophisticated criticisms of films or books are little more than adult versions of the name calling that happens in childhood. When someone writes, "I found his piece of poetry impermissibly obtuse," he may simply be using an adult way of saying, "I don't like you," or even, "You look kind of funny to me"—the sort of nastiness that is heard regularly on school playgrounds when the teacher is not looking. But the people in Psalm 120 are not only being nasty; they are being deceitful. They are saying things that are unkind, certainly, but more than simply being unpleasant, they are untrue. We do not know exactly who these people were who were speaking "lying deceit," but we do know it hurt the person who wrote the psalm.

## It Feels Like You Are in a Trap

The psalmist tells us that he is in "distress" (v. 1), a word that has the idea of a narrow or confined place. He is saying here that he was feeling trapped by others' words. That is exactly the feeling you get when someone lies about you or spreads deceit about you. This distress that he is talking about is no minor emotional bumped toe or scratched knee. The distress is the experience of being locked away. When someone launches a gossip campaign against you, the result of that can be to leave you feeling stuck or imprisoned. You feel that whatever you do from this point on will be interpreted in the light of what that person said about you.

If someone said that you were jealous, then told a story with just enough truth to make the charge of jealousy seem credible to those who were listening, from then on you would fear that saying anything even vaguely critical of any program or event will be taken in light of that comment. People might say to themselves as they listen to you, "Oh, he's just saying that because he's the jealous type." Or if someone noticed that you like to read Shakespeare rather than watch Oprah's latest TV channel, he might create a story about you that gives an impression that, frankly, you are a bit of a snob. So the next time you turn up at a meeting wearing a perfectly normal outfit, pleasant-looking though not particularly expensive, you might fear that everyone will be saying in their heads, "Look at that snob. Isn't she vain!"

Slander makes you feel like you are in a trap.

## It Feels Like You Have Been Shot

The psalmist tells us that they have a "deceitful tongue" (vv. 2–3). The word used for "deceit" here has the sense of *shooting*. He feels as if he is in the firing line. The psalm is not just describing someone saying something petty, an occasional sarcastic sneer perhaps. No, this is a little more clever than that, perhaps a bit more sinister. It is deliberate deceit, words aimed as carefully as a sniper aims. They are well-constructed lies. Someone or some group of people is picking up on things that the author of this psalm had said or done and then turning those things around to make him look bad. They are using his words as ammunition against him—shooting words.

This may not be slander in our modern legal sense of libel, but it is slander in the sense of lies spread around the community with the deliberate intention of causing harm, like a water-cooler conversation that you were not a part of but affects your reputation, or a few words shared about you for prayer in every prayer meeting in town, or a whisper in the ear of those who have the power to influence your career to make them look at you with disdain. If you have experienced anything like this, you know how damaging such deceit can be. You may have the wounds to show for it, wounds every bit as real as a bullet hole.

What can you do about it? After all, you probably do not know exactly what was said because you were unlikely to have been there when it was said. All you know is that you pick up a change in atmosphere when you walk into the room or a feeling that influences the tone when you are present. If you try to say anything about it, you will be guessing, and then it will be easy to characterize you as being paranoid as well. And if you happen by chance to hit the nail on the head about what is being said about you behind your back, then you can be characterized as nasty as well as vain. It feels like you are trapped in a box and cannot get out. It feels like you have taken a bullet and cannot stop the bleeding. What is the answer? As surprising as it may sound, the answer is to read this Psalm.

## A Strange Place to Start

At first glance it is strange that the Psalms of Ascent start with lies and deceit, but when you think about it, that actually is the most important and natural starting point. It dispenses once and for all with the rather unhelpful limerick I heard growing up as a child: "Sticks and stones may break my bones but words will never harm me." If only that were true; unfortunately, if someone calls you fat or ugly or stupid or lazy, it tends to hang over you for many, many years. Unaddressed, it can influence your entire life. So it is very important that we do good soul work to get rid of those lies and journey to the truth about ourselves in relation to God.

You may think talking about ourselves is hopelessly compromised in terms of pop psychotherapy, but it is interesting to me that in this psalm, one of the repeated refrains is directly related to the self. Deliver "me" he says (v. 2); even, perhaps rather self-indulgently, "woe to me" (v. 5). Both instances are talking about the self, and then the self in relation to this particular situation is brought by this distressed individual into the realm of God. He uses the first-person pronoun "I" a lot—this is not something about them or us, but about "me." He is making this personal, for it is personal, and he needs personal help.

## 1) Pray

> In my distress I called to the Lord,
> and he answered me.
> Deliver me, O Lord,
> from lying lips,
> from a deceitful tongue. (vv. 1–2)

How does he deal with this distress? First, he prays about it. "In my distress I called to the LORD" (v. 1). He does not first tell one of his friends about it ("Did you hear what so-and-so said about me?"). He does not first tell the local authority figure, whether boss or principal or lawyer. He needs help from God first of all. "In my distress I called to the LORD, and *he* answered me."

The right approach is first to pray. It is no good trying to deal with lies about you before you have gone first to God. You are too raw, too likely to lash out with a hurtful word yourself and then make everything even worse. Somehow you have to go to God first and deal with it with him. I will admit that this is far easier written on the page than done at home or in a small group or at work. You see, the psalm is not merely "praying about it" in some rote or traditional fashion. The author of the psalm is actually honest with God in his heart about the distress, about the lying lips and the deceitful tongue. That is difficult, because part of what makes deceitful lies such a trap is that you never want them repeated again, not to anyone, perhaps not even to God. If someone says to you that your work is no good, the last thing you want to do is tell someone else that someone said your work is no good. You want to keep it to yourself in your little box, in your "distress," in your narrow confine.

Understandable, though, as the desire is to keep the deceit as secret as you can, often that just makes it all worse. As William Blake wrote, "I was angry with my friend: I told my wrath, my wrath did end. I was angry with my foe: I told it not, my wrath did grow."[1] The poison eats away at you. Somehow you have to be honest enough—shall we say, brave enough—to start by telling God about it. I am not saying that is easy, but I am saying it is where you are going to find healing. That, at least, is the testimony of the person who wrote this psalm. "In my distress I called to the LORD, and he answered me" (v. 1), which allows him to become confident that God will "deliver" him (v. 2). He has gained the certainty that in God's sovereignty even lying lips will be turned to his deliverance.

---

[1] William Blake, "Songs of Innocence and Experience," in *A Poison Tree* (Minneapolis: Filiquarian, 2007), 89.

Would you like that deliverance? First pray. Go to God in prayer, and you will find that he has a deliverance plan even for slander. Perhaps not straight away from the malicious consequences of the lies that have been spread about you, but straight away from adding to the malignancy by spreading lies back. It takes strength to be someone who stops gossip rather than keeps on spreading it around, especially when the wounds are yours, not someone else's. And that sort of strength (deliverance) can be found only in God: "Deliver me."

## 2) Tell the Pain to God

The psalmist does not just go to God and ask him for help. Important as that is, having prayed about it, in the context of that prayer the psalmist unleashes the ugliness that the pain has caused in his own soul.

> What shall be given to you,
>     and what more shall be done to you,
>         you deceitful tongue?
> A warrior's sharp arrows,
>     with glowing coals of the broom tree! (vv. 3–4)

Honestly, I can't quite decide whether verses 3 and 4 are a confession of the psalmist's personal anger and wish to get back at the horrible so-and-so who has been so mean to him, or a prophetic denunciation of God's judgment, or even a description of the inevitable result for the person who told the lies. In the end you fall into your own trap, and it is worse for you than for your victim.

Usually it is said that these verses are some sort of prophetic denunciation, but I'm a little uncomfortable with that. There certainly are instances in the Bible of righteous anger, but I find, at least in my personal experience, that whatever little righteous anger I have is least likely to be purely righteous anger when the wrong done is against me. I suspect it is usually rather tarnished by unrighteous anger too. I see a little too much here of the personal vindictiveness that you would not expect from someone trying to fulfill the Old Testament mandate of loving your neighbor or of helping your enemy when his ox or donkey is in trouble—these sorts of teachings that were as much mandated in the Old Testament law as they were in the New Testament teaching of love for neighbor and enemy.

We know that judgment is coming on all those who sin and do not repent, but as the apostle Paul wrote, quoting from the Old Testament, "'Vengeance is mine, I will repay,' says the Lord. . . . If your enemy is hungry, feed him" (Rom. 12:19–20). I do not think the psalmist is "letting them have it" in his heart. His knee-jerk reflex to pray suggests a far too mature spirituality for that kind of childishness. But I do think the sting of his anger is being drawn out by God in prayer. You see, what happens when someone hurts you is only half the cruelty. The real danger is that you'll become someone like that and start to hurt other people in turn. That vicious cycle is the standard pattern, whether of verbal or physical abuse, unless the grace of God and the gospel of Jesus Christ intervene, as they do here.

Verses 3 and 4 are really a form of confession. The deceit is shooting at him, and now he wants God to shoot back at them with sharp arrows and with glowing coals of the broom tree, fiery darts that would not go out. The broom tree coals once lit, we are told by an ancient commentator, were known to last without going out for a very long time. He wants the deceit that others have spread about him to come down on them ten times worse, if not more. It is a confession.

It is also, of course, a kind of prediction. Proverbs is full of the reality that if we set traps for other people, in the end the trap falls upon us. That is the kind of world that God has created—sin eventually results in judgment even in the here and now and only grows toward final judgment. That Wisdom Literature understanding of the moral universe, the world in which we live, is in the background here, no doubt, but this psalm is not written to the person doing the lying. It is written by the victim of the lying. Somehow in this place, in verses 3 and 4, he has to get the emotions—the dark, even demonic emotions—to the surface and then take them to the only place where they can be safely dealt with, God himself.

When I start to talk like that, you can begin to see why so often the Psalms were used in the New Testament to point to the cross. Psalm 110 is frequently quoted in the New Testament for that purpose. One ancient Christian writer actually recommended that when someone is beginning to find out about Christianity, he read the Psalms before reading the New Testament, which may be stretching things a bit too far, but you will know what he meant when you read the Psalms carefully. They are not only the language of the soul, the spirituality of the heart; they are not just a spiritual form of psychotherapy; they are *theotherapy*. They are the place where the objective doctrine combines with the subjective experience, and the questions that this combustible fire raises are all answered at the cross of Jesus, where love and justice meet.

Let this psalm take you there. Take all the bitterness you have swallowed over time, as you have replayed in your heart the nasty things that have been said about you, and leave it in God's hands. That might mean saying some things about those experiences in the safety of your relationship with God that would be as equally eye-opening as what the psalmist wrote in verses 3 and 4. Between you and God have confidential dealings so that you can then emerge on the other side. It probably will not be a one-off experience, but it will be a lifetime journey—the journey of forgiveness not just seven times but seventy times seven, as Jesus put it, the journey of the truth that I need forgiving just as much as anyone who has lied about me.

## 3) Real Peace

The last thing the psalmist does is even more remarkable. Some songs are trite because they are overly triumphalistic, too certain that everything is always going to be fine, that the sun will always shine upon your steps, and that with a spoonful of sugar, no problem is too big. Of course, for Christians there is victory to come, and there will be a time when there is no more crying, because Christ has won the victory. But we live in the here and now without that victory finally and fully applied, and it can be rather demoralizing to be asked to try to live in a preachy world where everything is as easy as a perfectly constructed three-point sermon. That's not life. All we hear are the perfect victories, and how this person came out of sin into light, and how the other person got victory over this problem or that, or how that person's children were struggling but now they are thriving. Wonderful as those stories are, if that is all we hear, then there is a danger that we are not really braced for the reality of the next step in the ongoing journey. The Christian life is a pilgrimage, meaning it is a journey back to home, so however great the victories are here, however thrilling the adventures, we are still going *there*, and it is only there that we will find full satisfaction.

So as the psalm concludes, it ends in a way that no modern writer of a devotional book would conclude, nor any hymn writer, nor any therapist, or at least too few of all of the above. He concludes with a reality check:

> Woe to me, that I sojourn in Meshech,
>     that I dwell among the tents of Kedar!
> Too long have I had my dwelling
>     among those who hate peace.
> I am for peace,
>     but when I speak, they are for war! (vv. 5–7)

Hardly a good finale to a popular Christian devotional book! The "woe to me" suggests that the psalmist is not yet completely over his personal hurt. He has made progress, but he still seems to me to be taking too much pity on himself. "Woe to me"? "Come on!" I want to say to him. "God has delivered you. He has answered you. You are moving toward Jerusalem. You are on the great journey with God's people to the city of God!" And yet, if we are honest, "woe to me" is sometimes how we feel. It is not right. It is not best. But it is real.

Meshech and Kedar are places far distant from Israel, one along the Black Sea and the other in the Arabian tribal areas. Together they seem to function as the psalmist's feelings toward the sort of people who are lying about him. They were from Meshech and Kedar; they were Philistines and Barbarians! It is not exactly politically correct to call some of those with whom he was dwelling crass and Philistine barbarian hordes—not much better than Mongol invaders! But again this psalmist has not yet arrived. He is still on the journey.

Yes, he is on the journey, but still at the end he has made a highly significant, life-changing discovery. He says, "I am for peace" or literally, "I peace" or "I *shalom*." Peace is nowhere near where he was in verses 3 and 4! Then he wanted to get them back with warrior's sharp arrows and glowing coals of a broom tree. But now he is peace. He has realized the shalom of God, so his disposition to these invaders who have labeled him and lied about him and put him in a relational trap is now one of peace. He is leaving it up to God now. Any response he makes to their slander is now not vengeful but peaceful, for their good. That has not changed who they are yet. They are still for war. But he has left them in God's hands and taken the most important step in dealing with lies and slander, which is to be in the right place himself before God. He is no longer defined by the lies that people say about him. He is defined by the truth of what God says about him. He knows he cannot control their response. He has left that between them and God. He has given up his right to play judge, jury, and executioner all rolled into one. *I peace.*

A Song of Ascents.
I lift up my eyes to the hills.
    From where does my help come?
My help comes from the Lord,
    who made heaven and earth.
He will not let your foot be moved;
    he who keeps you will not slumber.
Behold, he who keeps Israel
    will neither slumber nor sleep.
The Lord is your keeper;
    the Lord is your shade on your right hand.
The sun shall not strike you by day,
    nor the moon by night.
The Lord will keep you from all evil;
    he will keep your life.
The Lord will keep
    your going out and your coming in
    from this time forth and forevermore.
—Psalm 121

# 2

# HELP

With the best will in the world there still comes a time when all of us must realize that at some point we simply need help. Perhaps really macho men do exist who have sufficient "true grit" never to shed a tear or cry out in the dark from fright. But I, for one, suspect that image has far more to do with fantasy than with reality, the myth of the unconquerable hero pulling himself up by his own bootstraps, facing adversity with a steely glint in his eye, Rambo-like. That myth is just that, a myth. Of course there have been great men and women who have shown us the extent to which the human spirit can face adversity and come through on the other side, but when you read the biographies of, say, a George Washington, or an Alexander the Great, what is remarkable is not so much that they did not need resources to accomplish what they accomplished, but that when they needed those resources they found them.

## Where Can You Find Help?

Where do you go when you need help? Perhaps you harbor a secret suspicion that it is not quite Christian or mature to admit that you ever need help. Maybe you remember that it was Benjamin Franklin who said, "God helps those who help themselves." For some of us, asking for help seems more like weakness than the tried and tested method of pulling yourself up by your own shoelaces. I certainly do not want to encourage any more blubbering wimpiness than we already have these days, a tendency to give way to what you feel in the mistaken impression that, because you feel it, it must be true. A fleeting short-lived feeling can merely indicate that you ate a rather bad lunch, that your hormones are temporarily out of balance, or that you are in the midst of a momentary mood swing. But there are more consistent feelings that could tell you that you need help.

The author of this psalm is crying out, "Help!" These psalms are all intended to give us the ability to manage our feelings so that they are brought into line with reality. In particular this psalm is intended to give us the resources to find help when that is what we need. Sometimes this psalm is called "The Traveler's Psalm," and indeed it has often been used to bless those who are going on a journey to assure them of God's watching care. Yet in another way all the Psalms of Ascent are actually traveling psalms in the sense that they take worshipers on a pilgrimage toward God, first used perhaps as the pilgrims went up to Jerusalem for one of the great festivals that you can read about in the Old Testament. Later perhaps they were adopted as the Jewish people returned from their exile to Babylon and sang these same psalms. It seems to me that they were designed by God to help us journey closer in our relationship to him and to avoid the many pitfalls and difficulties and diversions and distractions that can prevent us from continuing.

## Avoiding a Common Pitfall

One of the pitfalls that often comes on the spiritual journey is not being willing to ask for help. I love the sort of determination and spirit represented by Franklin's famous quotation about God helping those who help themselves. In a way, I wonder whether we need a little bit more of that and less of the attitude that "I have a right to receive help even though I've done nothing to deserve it." It reminds me a little of the poem by Rudyard Kipling called "If":

> If you can keep your head when all about you
> Are losing theirs and blaming it on you, . . .
> If you can meet with Triumph and Disaster
> And treat those two impostors just the same. . . .
> If you can fill the unforgiving minute
> With sixty seconds' worth of distance run,
> Yours is the Earth and everything that's in it,
> And—which is more—you'll be a Man, my son!

The message is that true manliness is a stoic persistence. Or, as Winston Churchill put it, "Never, never, never, give up." Maybe we do need a bit more of a Rocky Balboa attitude, getting up again when you have been knocked down and keeping on fighting. However, the reality is that God does not help those who help themselves. God helps those who know they need help. Ask and you will receive. Seek and you will find. Knock and the door will be opened (see Matt. 7:7; Luke 11:9).

## Taking the Initial Step of Looking Up for Help

The first step, the most remarkable step, that we find in this psalm is that he begins to look up for help.

> I lift up my eyes to the hills.
> From where does my help come? (v. 1)

Counselors all over the world will tell you that in some ways this step in the first verse is really the most important step to take, to acknowledge that there is something beyond your personal resources and that you need help with it. Pastors will say the same, especially when they are dealing with a clear habitual sin, a bondage that needs breaking. To come and say, "I need help with this," is a most important initial step. The idea that you can always fix everything yourself has caused the breakdown of more marriages, the heartbreak of more people, and the disaster of more businesses than perhaps any other idea on the face of the planet. Pride might be the first casualty of failure, but pride is also failure's common cause. "Pride goes before destruction, and a haughty spirit before a fall" (Prov. 16:18).

But if it is important to admit that we all need help from time to time, then it is also very important that we go to the right place to find help. Translations handle the second half of the first verse either as a question or a statement ("From where does my help come?" ESV; "from whence cometh my help," KJV). The difference partly depends on whether you think that the "hills" are appropriate places for help. Are they the hills surrounding Jerusalem as symbols of godliness, seen as the pilgrim gets closer to the end of his journey? Are they perhaps the hills that the weary soldier might look up to from the valley beneath, hoping that his Jewish brothers will ride over to his aid like the cavalry coming to rescue him? Or, more negatively, are the hills the high places where, throughout Israelite history, God's people were tempted to go back to Canaanite religion? We are not told one way or another clearly here. The point is that there is a natural tendency for all of us to glance skyward when we need assistance. We look *up* for help.

## Going Beyond the Hills

However, you must not stop at the hills. Nature is designed by nature's God to take you to its creator.

> My help comes from the Lord,
>    who made heaven and earth. (v. 2)

There is a place for natural diversion from stress—a thoughtful walk in the woods, an energizing hike up a hill to gain a mountaintop view of the situation. Such escapes from the burdens of life by enjoying creation are good in themselves and can be a timely relief. But nature is not the solution. Looking to the hills is a sign that you feel the need for help, but it is not the help that you need.

The perspective of mountain landscape is not the solution; it points to the solution. The problem with staying looking at the hills is that such escape can morph into escapism. People who stop at the hills can start to look for more permanent forms of escapism: quitting their job and going traveling, self-medicating with alcohol to dull the pain, constantly checking the scores of their favorite sports team on the Internet. Spectator sport may be so popular because it gives people a momentary escape from their real needs. The ancient Romans controlled the crowds through a combination of what was called "bread and circuses," that is, food and gladiator entertainment. Nowadays the entertainment is different, but the result still can distract us from our real needs. There is, of course, nothing wrong with an innocent bit of diversion, but we must go farther. The help is not in the hills; it is in the hills' God, the maker of heaven and earth.

## Focus on the Nature of God

Now we come to the part of the psalm where the first person (I) switches to the third person (he).

> He will not let your foot be moved;
>    he who keeps you will not slumber.

Behold, he who keeps Israel
will neither slumber nor sleep.
The LORD is your keeper . . . (vv. 3–5a)

The person talking, "I," is now addressed by someone else: "He will not let *your* foot be moved"; "He who keeps *you* will not slumber." We do not know exactly why this switch in voice takes place. Some scholars say it is an internal dialogue, as if the psalmist is talking to himself, saying, "Come on, now. Look to God. He won't let you down. Let me tell you why, self." In that view this is a poetic soliloquy, an internal dialogue recorded for other people to read. Other scholars think this part of the psalm was originally a choir singing antiphonally, that is, one group of singers answering the soloist with a response. The soloist begins, "I lift up my eyes to the hills. From where does my help come? My help comes from the LORD, who made heaven and earth." Then comes the choir responding with, "He will not let your foot be moved." And then perhaps the congregation joins in, "Behold, he who keeps Israel will neither slumber nor sleep." But whether this is self talk or a choir singing, it is a form of conversation designed to persuade you that looking to God is possible when you focus upon who God is, upon his nature.

In one sense you may think that this psalm is simply saying that when you need help, ask God. But unless that instruction is shored up with some rigorous theology, it becomes painfully trite, potentially damaging, and definitely discouraging. "Just trust God," someone can say, like a plaster applied to a hemorrhage. So the psalm does far more than offer simplistic piety. First, it says that this God is the maker of everything. So when you say, "Trust God," you are not saying, "Trust one of the *gods*." You are referencing Someone entirely different. He is the maker, not a spirit of the air who dances this way and that in accord with capricious fortune and at the whim of the dictates of earthly powers and natural events. No, he's the rock-solid creator of heaven and earth, all of reality. That is who he is.

Not only is he the creator; he is the covenant God. So verses 3 and 4 are saying, "You can be sure that God will not let your foot slip because this is the God who, in his covenant, has promised to look after his people." If you are one of his people, then he will look after you.

Jesus makes the same point when he tells the parable of the ninety-nine sheep and the one lost sheep. God is the God who will not let a single person of his people fall. So you may feel in your desperation, if you're being honest, that you are alone, that everyone else in church is fine. But God knows. And not only does he know; he also gave his blood for his people, and in dying for his people, he will never let you individually, as a part of his people, be snatched out of his hand. You can go to God for help. He is the creator. He is the covenant God. He is the watcher.

## God Is Watching over You

To apply the truth of God's nature to this need for help, the psalm begins to draw a vivid picture. Often your imagination needs to be reframed when you need help; you need to be able to see that God can help and picture that real help is possible. So the psalm says, "God is your keeper. He is your watcher." The word for "keep" runs through the rest of the psalm, and the word for "watch" has the same root. The two ideas are connected. God is *keeping* you, he is *watching* over you, he is *looking* after you. The picture is of God standing guard, eyes open, neither slumbering nor sleeping. It is a powerful image.

One of the difficulties of trusting God enough to ask him for help is that you cannot see God. That is sometimes why people watch TV rather than pray, or why they go out and party rather than pray, or even why they go and talk to someone else instead of pray. God cannot be seen. But what if he sends word that *he sees you*? That is what happened when God's people were slaves in Egypt. The Bible tells us that "God saw" their need (Ex. 2:25). The Old Testament priestly blessing, that in some ways this psalm reflects over and over again, emphasizes the same point: "The LORD bless you and *keep* you; the LORD make his *face* to shine upon you and be gracious to you; the LORD lift up his *countenance* upon you and give you peace" (Num. 6:24–26). He's *looking*.

Of course, we live by faith, not by sight, but God does not. He sees. The image is a bit like a child reassured who has been afraid to go to sleep. The parent says, "Don't worry. I'll stay in the room tonight and watch over you." God is saying, "I am watching over you." We can sleep because God does not. We can travel because God knows the way. We can keep going because God will not let our foot slip. He is constantly watching.

## God Is Your Shade

The psalmist uses one other metaphor, that of shade:

> The LORD is your shade on your right hand.
> The sun shall not strike you by day,
>     nor the moon by night. (vv. 5b–6)

In the Middle East the sun is dangerous. The heat can be blinding, and sunstroke can kill, so shade is a dramatic picture of God's protection. God is your shade "on your right hand," the right hand being the place in battle where you needed protecting, because the shield was held in the left hand.

It is easy to understand the metaphor of protection from the sun, but what of protection from the "moon by night"? Some people explain this by saying that the moon was believed to have potentially deranging effects on people. In a couple of places in the New Testament "moon-struck" is a literal translation of the description of epilepsy (Matt. 4:24; 17:15). We have the remains of the same idea when we use the term *lunatics*. That word originally meant those who have succumbed to the malign influence of the lunar rays of the moon. A more likely explanation, though, it seems to me, is that this is again picture language of the dangers of traveling by day (sunstroke) and the dangers of traveling by night (bandits, thieves, robbers). The psalm is saying that God is a protection against the dangers of the day and of the night.

## No Evil

As the psalm comes to its beautiful poetic conclusion, it leaves a series of questions that I find troubling. Verses 7 and 8 conclude with a total promise for complete protection in every way at all times and in all places forever.

> The LORD will keep you from all evil;
>> he will keep your life.
> The LORD will keep
>> your going out and your coming in
>> from this time forth and forevermore. (vv. 7–8)

Really? No evil? Now and always? Not a single little bit?

Dietrich Bonhoeffer was killed at the end of the Nazi regime for his part in an assassination attempt on the life of Hitler. Bonhoeffer was a pastor and author, and his life is championed in many places as an example of Christian sacrifice. But in the light of this psalm, in what sense did God watch over Bonhoeffer's life? In what way was he kept from "all evil"? No doubt you can read the famous chapter 8 of Paul's letter to the Romans in the New Testament and say that all things work together for the good of those who love him. So you can say that Bonhoeffer may have lost his life, but his life was used by God remarkably, and he now has eternity to enjoy God. He did not lose out. I have no difficulty with that concept. Indeed, many times you can see, as Tertullian said, that "the blood of the martyrs is the seed of the church." Suffering is not to be thought of as counter to God's purposes but as a part of God's purposes. How can Christians believe in the crucifixion of the Son of God if they do not believe that God has a plan for suffering? We worship the king with the crown of thorns, not the golden tiara.

Such ideas about suffering are difficult yet coherent. But this psalm not only says what Romans 8 says, that all things will work together for the good of those who love God; this psalm says that nothing evil will happen. Are we then to believe that the death of a martyr is not truly or finally evil? I think the answer to that must be yes. There are worse things than dying. There are worse things than losing your job. There are worse things than finding your most precious relationship is breaking down. There are worse things than being hurt. But even that is not quite what the psalm is saying, for it says "all evil," not "there are worse things than that kind of harm."

Think of the surgeon prepping himself to go into surgery. As he prepares, he knows in one sense that he is about to do his patient harm. He is going to cut open his body and delve in with surgical tools. The patient will bleed. If there were no anesthetic, the patient would be screaming in pain strapped to the operating bed. That sounds evil. Yet that surgeon rightly believes that he is following the Hippocratic Oath to "do no harm." Harm is not harm when it good does.

That is what I think the psalm must be saying. Yes, this may hurt. That is why you are asking for help. Look at the hills, but do not stop there. Go beyond them. Look to the God who made the mountains, who made everything.

But you may say, "What does he care?" If you are a Christian, you commit your life to Jesus; you are a part of God's people, and God has promised—and sealed that promise with his own blood—to take care of his people, to look after them, to watch, to see, and to therefore guard. He is a shade protecting you from the heat of the work of the noonday sun and the anxiety and fears of the moonlit night.

But you say, "Will that really work in all situations, in all circumstances? You don't understand what I'm going through!" Will it work not just then but even now in our modern world with our modern temptations and difficulties and not just now but as far as the human temporal horizon can see—tomorrow, and tomorrow, and tomorrow's tomorrow, and forever?

And the psalmist says, "Yes, it will work." There may be painful things. The psalmist knows that otherwise he would not be writing this psalm asking for help from painful things. There may be painful things, but if you entrust yourself to God, then you will never experience any final or true evil. And that might take some redefinition of evil for you to believe. But then who is the one truly in harm's way? Is it the miser atop his mountain of gold, dragonish gleam of avarice in his eye as he destroys his life from the inside out? Or is it the child of God making his joyful journey with a song in his heart and a tune on his lips as he walks step by step closer to the eternal joy of the crucified Savior?

I know which I will choose. What about you? Or as the psalm might say, "Where are you going to go when you need help?"

A Song of Ascents. Of David.
I was glad when they said to me,
    "Let us go to the house of the Lord!"
Our feet have been standing
    within your gates, O Jerusalem!
Jerusalem—built as a city
    that is bound firmly together,
to which the tribes go up,
    the tribes of the Lord,
as was decreed for Israel,
    to give thanks to the name of the Lord.
There thrones for judgment were set,
    the thrones of the house of David.
Pray for the peace of Jerusalem!
    "May they be secure who love you!"
Peace be within your walls
    and security within your towers!"
For my brothers and companions' sake
    I will say, "Peace be within you!"
For the sake of the house of the Lord our God,
    I will seek your good.
—Psalm 122

# 3

# CHURCH

If you go to God's house, many thoughts may enter your head, but I wonder whether one of them is, "This is almost as exciting as falling in love"? The feeling of falling in love is in a Taylor Swift song, the poetry of *Romeo and Juliet*, or the buzz of Valentine's Day, but it is rarely what people think of when they go to church.

## Falling in Love

Falling in love may not be all that it is cracked up to be. Psychologist M. Scott Peck, in *The Road Less Traveled*, described falling in love as simply the breaking down of the "ego boundaries" that normally give two people the sense that they are separate.[1]

Ironically, Peck felt, people give up on love if they no longer feel in love, when at that moment real love has the chance to begin. I have a lot of sympathy with the idea that our culture puts too much weight on falling in love. What happens when the initial buzz fades and you feel like you have fallen out of love? Is love precarious, like a tree you climb that, with one slip, you can fall out of? Or is love more of a commitment, like a sacrifice? I meet those who have been damaged by falling in (and out of) love, who have found that if you remove commitment from falling in love, what you are left with is sex. I suppose then, if we did a word association game with the word *love*, many today would associate it with sex. People *make* love (or, given that the term *love* seems too fragile, just have friends with benefits). Still, love in the right sense, perhaps also falling in love if it leads to real love, is the greatest (1 Cor. 13:13). And how many would associate that love with the word *church* or with God's house?

---

[1] M. Scott Peck, *The Road Less Traveled* (New York: Simon & Schuster, 1978), n.p.

## Love Church

This psalm makes that association. It says, "May they be secure who *love* you" (v. 6). The word "love" there probably originally carried the overtones of the love of a husband for a wife, although it was also used more broadly of many other kinds of love. It is not a dictionary definition of love that makes me think the author of the psalm is head over heels in love with God's house. It is the whole style of his poetry which reads like a love poem. He is excited. He is thrilled. He is bubbling over. "Our feet have been standing within your gates, O Jerusalem!" (v. 2). "Wow! I'm standing at her door, and I'm trying to find the courage to ring the doorbell! Look at Jerusalem. How wonderfully built. It is all so fantastic. Look at her. Isn't she stunning?" Jerusalem here is very much a "she" that he is loving.

That is very important today because our tendency is to love in a self-orientated way. If we love someone, we tend to love him or her as long as we are receiving what we want or feel that we need from that one. But what if there is a love we can experience that is meant to be for the benefit of each, even at the loss of ourselves? Erich Fromm, in his *The Sane Society*, wrote, "There is not much love to be found in human relations of our day. There is rather a superficial friendliness. . . . There is also a good deal of subtle distrust."[2] *Superficial friendliness.* A "hale fellow well met." A "glad hand." Because of this superficiality, we long for community. The technological revolution allows us to talk with people all around the world through social media and have friends in other countries and in other places and connect immediately. We are in a high-tech reality beyond that which we could have conceived a few short years ago. But at the same time, we also long for what someone has called a "high touch" reality. As we see revolutions in the news, fueled to some extent by the communication of Facebook and Twitter, they still congregate in the central city square.

## Finding Community

When it comes to church, surprisingly, we can miss out on community. As Keith Miller asserts:

---

[2] Erich Fromm, *The Sane Society* (New York: Rinehart, 1955), 135.

Churches today are filled with people who outwardly look contented and at peace but are inwardly crying out for someone to love them. . . . Confused, frustrated, guilty, and often unable to communicate even within their own families. But the other people in the church look so happy and contented, that one seldom has courage to admit his own deep needs.[3]

I want you to have the courage to admit your deepest needs for community. In Psalm 121 the psalmist looked up to the hills to find help from God. Now in Jerusalem he seems convinced that he will find a community love. That is the sense of the poetry, almost (to make it doggerel), "roses are red, violets are blue, my God is good, my church is too."

The author of the psalm is clearly not like one of those people who loves God but is not too sure about the church. For him, as in the New Testament too, God and his people are intimately connected. *Extra ecclesiam nulla salus* is the ancient phrase, that is, "no salvation outside of the church"—a principle that can be misunderstood to mean that the church saves you, but really it means that *if* you are saved (by grace through faith alone), *then* you will be a part of the church. A person of God who is not a part of the people of God is a strange anomaly. Kevin DeYoung and Ted Kluck have coined a new term for describing this "grotesque anomaly," as John Stott called it. They say that if *decapitation*, from the Latin word *caput*, means "to cut off the head," then it stands to reason that *decorpulation*, from the Latin word *corpus*, should refer to the cutting off of the body. In other words, if there are some churches that tend not to listen to Jesus through his Word and are therefore in danger of decapitation from Christ, then there are some Christians who tend to live disconnected from the church who are in danger of decorpulation from Christ's body.

## 1) Resist Individualism

How do we begin to love church (or to love church more)? The psalmist first resists individualism:

---

[3] Keith Miller, *The Taste of New Wine* (Waco, TX: 1965), 71.

> I was glad when they said to me,
>> "Let us go to the house of the LORD!"
> Our feet have been standing
>> within your gates, O Jerusalem! (vv. 1–2)

Individualism may be a particular problem of our time, but individuals have always needed to embrace godly community. Look at how the ancient psalmist approached community: "I" (as an individual) "was glad" (excited or thrilled) "when they" (the godly friends) "said to me" (the individual), "Let us" (now he and they are *us*, united as a community) "go to the house of the LORD!" And so "our feet" arrive "within your gates."

That means that when I say, "Let's go to church," you are glad and you go. You don't think, "Oh, that means I miss some extra sleep," or, "I won't be able to watch the game on TV." You are glad, excited, thrilled, motivated. Church may not be meant to be entertaining in the sense of empty of meaningful content, but it is certainly not meant to be boring! It is something that is intended to make you glad.

### All God's People

This community is also for all God's people, all "the tribes":

> Jerusalem—built as a city
>> that is bound firmly together,
> to which the tribes go up,
>> the tribes of the LORD,
> as was decreed for Israel,
>> to give thanks to the name of the LORD. (vv. 3–4)

Church is a tent big enough for all God's people. There are different tribes with different styles and tastes, but all gather for church. Part of resisting individualism is resisting the natural human tribalism that makes you want to club together only with people like you. Church is bigger than that. It is God's house, not my faction's rallying point; God's Word, not my theological axe to grind; the Lord's Table, not my private dinner for my group. Some refine their theological distinctives to the nanoparticle level so that the only ones with whom they could go to church would be themselves, and even they might not be quite sound.

"If you find a perfect church don't join it; you'll only spoil it" is a phrase with enough pepper to sneeze the Pharisee out of most Christians. The reality is none of us is easy to love, but in loving each other we resist the hell of individualism. As Dostoevsky put it, "I maintain that [hell] is the suffering of being unable to love." Church is a drug rehab center where narcissists like you and me learn to kick the habit, a new society for the new creation.

So, the first part of this psalm is a very clear rejection of any individualistic notion of what it means to have a relationship with God. Me, my God, my Bible, and my Starbucks latte is not the people of God. Me and my two friends reading the Bible in my basement is not God's people getting together. It may be true, as Keith Green said, that "going to church does not make you a Christian any more than going to McDonald's makes you a hamburger," but if you are looking for a Big Mac, McDonald's is the place to go. There may perhaps be sheep without the house as well as wolves within the house. But to be a part of the universal people of God, you are by definition a part of the local people of God. Otherwise it is like saying we love everyone in general without actually loving anyone in particular. You cannot love the people of God if you are not loving any particular people of God.

## 2) Reject Cynicism

Second, not only does the psalmist resist the individualism that keeps one away from God's house, but he also rejects cynicism about God's house once he arrives:

> There thrones for judgment were set,
>    the thrones of the house of David. (v. 5)

It is easy to be cynical about the local church, the tradition of a particular Christian group, or the idiosyncrasies of a "Jesus is my homeboy" trendy worship service. The "thrones" (v. 5), "walls" (v. 7), and "towers" (v. 7) can seem impersonal, institutional, sterile, and even just downright silly. Strangely, though, the author of the psalm seems just as excited about the well-built walls and the thrones for judgment as he is about the friends with whom he is glad to go to church.

It is easy to be cynical about traditional religion, but the psalmist seems thrilled by this veteran faith of walls and towers and thrones. Cynicism can be about authority figures, but this psalmist admires the judgment thrones from which justice is administered. There is no sneering, "Oh, David *would* praise the throne of King David, wouldn't he?" but a genuine gladness in the good authority of the ruler. Reading this childlike love for God's house contrasts starkly with those church-weary Christians who have "seen behind the curtain" and find it hard to take it all seriously anymore. While some things that churches do would make a cynic of a saint, could it be that cynicism about God's house sometimes masks cynicism about God? One person says, "I love Jesus, but when I go to church I smirk behind my hand." But if the church is the bride of Christ, how is that different from saying, "I love my friend, but when I see his wife I giggle"? If you love Jesus, you will not be cynical about his bride—disappointed at times, wanting to change it often, but not cynical.

Cynicism put into extreme practice is dramatically told in Shakespeare's play *King Lear*. The king gives his daughters their inheritance only to discover that having got what they wanted, they then feel free to treat him with gross ingratitude. The old man ends up roofless in the wilds in the middle of a raging storm. He bitterly shouts, "Blow, blow, thou winter wind. Thou art not so unkind as man's ingratitude." It is too easy to be cynical about the church without realizing what it has given us or the bitterness that such cynicism can cause to those who have gone before us.

### Praying for Peace

The psalmist has none of that ingratitude. He has resisted the form of cynicism that grabs what you want and will not let anyone else tell you otherwise. Instead, the psalmist even admires the thrones for judgment, the justice and authority of God's house. He rejects cynicism about authority as he urges us to pray for peace:

> Pray for the peace of Jerusalem!
>    "May they be secure who love you!
> Peace be within your walls
>    and security within your towers!" (vv. 6–7)

Without any thrones for judgment, or justice, fairness, and order, there can be no peace in God's house. It is fairly straightforward to resist individualism and embrace the community of God's people, because you know you are not meant to be alone. It takes a little more work to reject cynicism about the authority of God, because no one likes to be told what to do. But what if God's authority loves to give us peace? The word *peace*, you see, does not mean merely the absence of war, but it means the presence of wholeness, of *shalom*. "Love is sparingly soluble in the words of men," Oliver Wendell Holmes said, meaning that love is difficult to define.[4] But God's love, our love for his people, his loving order and justice, all cause the psalmist to pray for this wholeness expressed in the word *shalom*.

### Hope for the Church

Finally, he rejects cynicism about the future of God's house:

> For my brothers and companions' sake
> I will say, "Peace be within you!"
> For the sake of the house of the LORD our God,
> I will seek your good. (vv. 8–9)

His commitment is one more chapter in the ongoing narrative of Jerusalem. You first find the city of Jerusalem as the home of Melchizedek, the priest-king whose meaning is told in full in the New Testament book of Hebrews. Then the story of Jerusalem goes underground for a while until you meet it once more when the Israelites take over the land and Jerusalem is the citadel of the Jebusites, which they called Jebus. Initially Jerusalem was such a strong location that it was not captured, and the tribe of Benjamin settled for the Jebusites' living within the fortress until David took over the city and it became known as the City of David. He brought the ark of the covenant there, and David's son Solomon built the temple.

God's people did not stay faithful, and despite many warnings from the prophets they gave in to idolatry and went into exile, to return many years later, as God had promised, to rebuild the temple. The sight

---

[4] "The Autocrat of the Breakfast Table," in *The Works of Wendell Holmes* (Boston: Phillips, Sampson, 1858), 271.

thrilled some and made others weep for disappointment when they remembered the glories of the old temple. They were a people in captivity still under foreign power despite the brief reign of the Maccabees. Then under King Herod, a vassal king for the Roman Empire, the temple was built up again to some form of magnificence.

And, of course, it was to this temple that Jesus came, this city into which Jesus walked. Perhaps you remember the scene as he looked out over Jerusalem and said, "Would that you, even you, had known on this day the things that make for peace! But now they are hidden from your eyes" (Luke 19:42). Jesus is referring to Psalm 122:8. Jesus loved them, and he wanted to win them, but they rejected and crucified him, in God's sovereign plan. As Jesus said, "Greater love has no one than this, that someone lay down his life for his friends" (John 15:13).

Jerusalem continued to dream of a material kingdom of military power, attempted to throw off the rule of Rome, and was sacked and the temple destroyed, and then it happened again, and the Israelite people were expelled. One day the Jerusalem that is above will be revealed, the spiritual Jerusalem of which we who believe in Jesus all partake, and of which we as part of Jesus are a part of that master story.

There is no room for cynicism in such a story of the future as we trace the dots through the narrative of the Bible, only for the seeking of the good of God's people, his church all around the world. It is a love story. "Come, I will show you the Bride, the wife of the Lamb. And he carried me away in the Spirit to a great, high mountain, and showed me the holy city Jerusalem coming down out of heaven from God, having the glory of God, its radiance like a most rare jewel, like a jasper, clear as crystal" (Rev. 21:9–11).

So every time you are tempted to feel fed up with church, or cynical about God's people, or say to yourself, "Why do I need all these people? Why can't I just get along by myself?" look at this psalm. Look at how the author feels about God's people, how he rejects individualism and cynicism, and how it leads to this story of the future peace. Then seek the church's good, her prosperity, her wholeness. Every time you are tempted to feel unloved or unlovable, think what it would be like to be part of a group for whom God himself would come down, would live, would die, and would rise again in order that we might have peace, wholeness now and evermore.

Yes, every trembling instinct, every longing romance, every hopeful glance, every happy long-lasting relationship is a mere glimmer, a mere shadow, a mere echo of *the* Love Story. If you want to know how to make your wife happy, treat her like this. If you want to know how to make your man happy, respond like this. Even more importantly, if you want to make God happy, love his people, for that is the center of his heart. After all, his valentine was not cheap or tawdry, commercialized or trite, but rugged—even bloody—where all his disappointment toward his people and all his people's betrayals were sacrificed and dealt with to win peace. If that doesn't make you a little bit happy, I don't know what will.

A SONG OF ASCENTS.
To you I lift up my eyes,
    O you who are enthroned in the heavens!
Behold, as the eyes of servants
    look to the hand of their master,
as the eyes of a maidservant
    to the hand of her mistress,
so our eyes look to the LORD our God,
    till he has mercy upon us.
Have mercy upon us, O LORD, have mercy upon us,
    for we have had more than enough of contempt.
Our soul has had more than enough
    of the scorn of those who are at ease,
    of the contempt of the proud.
—Psalm 123

# 4

# INJUSTICE

I will evermore be someone marked by an experience of injustice. I did not grow up in the ghetto, and I have never experienced the cold horror of racism, nor am I like the countless millions who struggle in slums slick with human waste. I am a white Westerner with a privileged background and a privileged education. I did not have to fight my way up from the ground, earn my living sieving through garbage as some do, grateful for the job. I have not begged, as a blinded untouchable, for a living. I have rarely felt the systemic repression of structural evil that makes us immune to the possibility that we might make a better life for ourselves and leaves the downtrodden with the hangdog look that cannot accept their fate or believe that things will ever be different. I have not been homeless on the streets for years, hunted for shelter under a bridge, or hidden from the prying eyes around through the easy numbness of the bottle. I have known people who have been in these situations, and I have done my bit from time to time to alleviate what suffering I could.

## Compassion

As such, I have felt myself to be a compassionate person, not one likely to pass by on the other side but to reach out a hand to those who have been the victim of scorn or contempt from those who are at ease. My brush with injustice was far more minor than what we read about and watch and what millions experience today. It is so minor I dare not mention it in the same breath as I mention the tortured or the repressed. When we look at Egypt or Tunisia or Libya today, we hear stories of people who have experienced injustices of the sort that few of us can imagine and fewer of us still have even come close to suffering. Our petty injustices must not be put at the same level as someone who by virtue of birth in a shantytown on the outskirts of some megapolis in the Majority World has only one chance in a million of getting out, the sort of fantasy escape that the movie *Slumdog Millionaire* dramatized. Our injustices are utterly worthless beside such stories, except for one thing: they allow us to extrapolate. They allow us the ability to gain a little empathy. They allow us the grace of understanding and perhaps not simply sporadic compassion but divine mercy.

## Empathy

It is one thing to look at a picture of a starving boy, or to meet a child whose parents have died of AIDS, or to hear the story of someone who was tortured during the civil rights movement. It is another thing to believe that it could have been you, and to put yourself in that person's shoes, and to realize that you and he are made of the same dust and by the same creator.

That's what my one little brush with injustice has done for me; it has allowed me to feel the sheer anger of being wrongly accused, of being victimized. Of having those who are at ease oppress and dominate, sometimes using moral words to encourage their oppression. The Yale professor of philosophy Nicholas Wolterstorff, in his book on justice, wrote about his observations regarding the rationale that was presented to keep on repressing people in the apartheid regime in South Africa. "I saw, as never before, the good overwhelming the just, and benevolence and the appeal to love being used as instruments of oppression." He carried on, "Oppressors do all they can to cast the situation in terms of better and worse rather than justice and injustice, in terms of good behavior and bad behavior, in terms of benevolence."[1] I certainly experienced that, and that was the point of the dagger—not just the oppression but that the oppression was good for you.

## A Larger Message

This psalm does not deal with all the issues related to justice, nor can we. Those issues are very great and intellectually complicated and prac-

---

[1] Nicholas Wolterstorff, *Justice: Rights and Wrongs* (Princeton, NJ: Princeton University Press, 2010), *vii–viii.*

tically strewn with pitfalls on that path to make sure that helping does not end up hurting. In the Western intellectual tradition, from Plato in his *Republic*, to Aristotle in his *Ethics*, to the work of Locke in the Enlightenment, to contemporary philosophers such as Rawls and economists such as Amartya Sen, various important distinctions are made. In some ways the simplest definition of justice is the most ancient, given by the Roman Justinian's codification of Roman law that justice is a steady and enduring will to render to each their just deserts, what is right.[2] What that right is has been much debated. For Plato it was the world of forms, that is, what is right is what is the Right (uppercase R), the idea of being Right that is behind our apparent right. For Locke and the Enlightenment tradition there were certain "unalienable rights" (as Thomas Jefferson put it) inherent to each human being. I am touching on extremely complex issues, but they are as nothing compared to the difficulty of making sure that whatever help that is given is not doing more damage than good. There is a difference between relief and development, and relief should not be given to those who need development or vice versa.

This psalm itself does not do more than touch on that sort of discussion, nor is it the fullest representative of the theme of justice in the Bible. We could go to the prophet Amos for that: "Let justice roll down like waters, and righteousness like an ever-flowing stream" (Amos 5:24); or to Isaiah's famous denunciation of Old Testament religion without practical care for the oppressed as something that God hates and is detestable to him, saying to them, "Seek justice, correct oppression; bring justice to the fatherless, plead the widow's cause" (Isa. 1:17).

We could look at Jesus's pronouncement that he had come to "proclaim good news to the poor" (Luke 4:18) and listen to most scholars who say that the poor there mean not only the economic . . . poor or the spiritual poor but the poor as those who are on the outside of God's people, to whom Jesus had come to appeal. We could look at Jesus's declaration that "as you did it to one of the least of these my brothers, you did it to me" (Matt. 25:40), meaning those brothers and sisters

---

[2] Ibid., 22.

of his in prison and suffering, Christians persecuted and victimized around the world and at home.

We could trace the Bible's story through this theme, and if you want to do that, you might read Craig Blomberg's *Neither Poverty nor Riches: A Biblical Theology of Possessions.*[3]

We could think of how the New Testament church in Acts, when it is described as having no poor among them (Acts 4:34), is fulfilling the Old Testament call to have no poor in the land so that the New Testament church is a representative now of God's plan for community. We could think of how difficult this was for the church, and how they set up various rules and procedures for caring for the poor widows, Paul advising Timothy that the widows on the list must meet certain qualifications of godliness and commitment to the church (1 Tim. 5:3–16).

We could think of how the Bible encourages the church to keep the main thing the main thing, to center on the Word and prayer, thereby not denying the prophetic voice to injustices or prudent involvement in matters of witness to Christ through care, and discuss all the tricky decisions this might from time to time bring before the elders and pastors.

But this psalm does something different. It is all rather more personal and frank and heartfelt than that. I want you to notice several things about it.

### 1) Submission

First, I want you to notice that radical submission to God is not at the opposite end of the spectrum from a desire to be free from oppression. The psalmist is submitting to God like a servant. He is groveling, we might say. He is looking to the master; she is looking to her mistress like an ancient chattel looked to the hand, waiting for the merest gesture to obey immediately. Our contemporary world tends to say that if you want to be free from repression, it starts with freeing yourself from submission to God. This psalm says the reverse. The only way to be free from repression is to have a higher set of values.

I think of Martin Luther King's interview when he was being criti-

---

[3] Craig Blomberg, *Neither Poverty nor Riches: A Biblical Theology of Possessions* (Grand Rapids, MI: Eerdmans, 1999).

cized for his opposition to the Vietnam War. He was asked on television whether he regretted that his stance might have alienated Lyndon Johnson, the president at the time. His reply was that loyalty should not be associated always with agreement, and that the principles of right and wrong in his conscience were the values to which he must hold true.

Unless we have a set of firm principles, we will not be able to stand up to naked power. And such principles are only secure when they are rooted in the person of God. The psalmist is not saying that he's groveling before a hard taskmaster; he's saying that because he is submitting to God in a radical way, he is able to stick to his principles. Think of your situation at work. If there is a chance to make a fast buck or two, will you cave in? If you have a radical submission to God and his Word, you will not. You have a higher loyalty.

## 2) Mercy, Not Justice

Second, I want you to notice that what the psalmist asks for is not justice but mercy. He certainly could have asked for justice. He has suffered contempt. He has had "more than enough of scorn." This scorn comes from those who, adding insult to injury, are "at ease"; they have no idea of the situation in which he has found himself personally and so are like an able-bodied person scorning a disabled person—they are doing something not just wrong but gross. The contempt comes from those who are proud; they not only think too little of the psalmist; they think too much of themselves. They prune their feathers while they spit at him. He certainly has room for wanting some justice. And at a human level, before other humans he would have room for justice. But not before God. No one in his right mind ever goes to God and says, "Give me justice before you." There is the cry that rightly goes up to God for justice, and that justice God promises his people will get; but before God, all of us must ask for mercy. None of us is righteous, not even one; before God what we are looking for is mercy.

Together those seem to be the two principles that you find in this prayer: mercy and submission. Together they are freeing. There is a revolutionary submission. The context of this psalm is quite possibly that of Ezra and Nehemiah and the rebuilding of the wall after the return from exile. Whether this psalm was written then or written earlier and used then, it is quite possible—not certain, but possible—that the psalm was employed in the context of the ridicule that Nehemiah and the people received at their attempted rebuilding of the wall. Their enemies were saying that the wall was going to cave in, that it was going to fall down, that it was a pathetic attempt at construction, and that they had no chance whatsoever. They were treating God's people with contempt. In such contexts it would have been easy for Nehemiah to lash back and attack. Instead he submitted to God. God is in charge. This is not just the doctrine of God's sovereignty; it is a personal decision to entrust the matter into the hands of the master, to look at his "hand" and let him be God in the situation.

## Looking to God

> To you I lift up my eyes,
>     O you who are enthroned in the heavens!
> Behold, as the eyes of servants
>     look to the hand of their master,
> as the eyes of a maidservant
>     to the hand of her mistress,
> so our eyes look to the LORD our God,
>     till he has mercy upon us. (vv. 1–2)

How much is that needed in so many situations when we feel repressed or wrongly treated! We tend to want to take the situation into our own hands and exact vengeance. We move purely at the human level and begin legal proceedings. We are not able to submit to the danger of letting God be God in the moment of trial and scorn. In Amartya Sen's technical work on justice, he begins with an illustration from Charles Dickens's *Great Expectations*: "In the little world in which children have their existence, there is nothing so finely perceived and finely felt, as injustice."[4] Your issue of repression could go back many years to your own childhood: a slight from your parents; an overlook of what was rightly yours; a brother or sister who treated you badly. It could be more recent: an injustice you perceive in some personal relationship. Deal with it by lifting your eyes up to heaven, not by fixing your eye

---

[4] Charles Dickens, *Great Expectations* (Mineola, NY: Dover, 2001), *vii*.

on the injustice. Practice a radical submission to God and his ways. As Spurgeon puts it, "We need not speak in prayer; a glance of the eye will do it all."[5] In this looking up to God, we meet not the eyes of another terrible dictator but the God of justice and mercy, compassion and grace, who looks tenderly on his people. Perhaps there is some job that you feel should have been yours, some opportunity that you have been denied. Look to God about it. The commentator Cox calls this "*oculus sperans*," "the eye of hope."[6]

## Pleading for Mercy

When the eyes fasten upon God, then the words gush out:

> Have mercy upon us, O Lord, have mercy upon us,
>     for we have had more than enough of contempt.
> Our soul has had more than enough
>     of the scorn of those who are at ease,
>     of the contempt of the proud. (vv. 3–4)

If the context is the time of Nehemiah under oppression, they prayed and did not retaliate, and then having given the matter to God, they went on with their work of building the wall. Sometimes God's reply can be delayed. Martin Luther describes the right attitude to such delay of our cry for mercy like this:

> For in that he defers his help, he does it not because he will not hear us, but to exercise and stir up our faith, and to teach us that the ways whereby he can and does deliver us are so manifold and miraculous, that we are never able to conceive them. Therefore let us think that the thing which we ask is not denied, but deferred, and assure ourselves that we are not neglected because of this delay.[7]

## Becoming the Change

Perhaps all this seems rather small by comparison with the massive issues of justice, of contempt and scorn, and of repression in our world today—in Libya and Egypt and Tunisia and among the millions starv-

---

[5] Charles Spurgeon, "Psalm 123," in *The Treasury of David* (public domain).

[6] Samuel Cox, *The Pilgrim Psalms: An Exposition of the Songs of Degrees* (London: Randolph, 1874), 56.

[7] Martin Luther, *A Commentary on the Psalms Called Psalms of Degrees* (London, 1819), 116.

ing. But no prayer is small, because prayer is directed to the God of all. My personal relationship with Jesus at a time of repression is the opportunity then to be changed by him and so to become what Gandhi called "the change that you wish to see in the world."

I like the African proverb that says that if you think you are too small to make a difference, try spending the night in a closed room with a mosquito. This is a mosquito prayer. It is buzzing around the Psalms, making its way to God, crying out over and over again for mercy. And in so doing, the psalmist, perhaps in the context of Nehemiah, is stopped from trying to take revenge and so appear petty and pathetic and exposed as far less powerful than his adversaries. Instead he goes to God, whose solution is far more powerful than any human pride.

## Pleading for Mercy for Others

We can pray mercy for ourselves. We can also pray mercy for other people, for those who are suffering contempt at the hands of oppressors. There are great temptations that come with being oppressed. We can make justice at a human level everything. We can take the gospel and turn it into a social action movement. We can, as T. S. Eliot said, end up doing the right thing for the wrong reasons, which he called "the last temptation," and "the greatest heresy."[8] In the end, speculations about justice and our attempts to achieve it are always fraught with difficulties, for we are bargaining between two sinners, caught in a mesh of depravity, and what we need is justice on a God level and mercy from the hands of the living Lord. It is no small thing that Christians learn to plead for mercy and to practice it as well, to embody the change they wish to see in the world.

## A Historical Example

One young Jewish man grew up in Germany 150 years ago, and the life of his family centered on the synagogue. The family became Protestant so that the father could practice law because of an edict banning Jews from taking the bar. Imagine that young man growing up and one day wondering why they were Protestant. Imagine an answer from the fa-

---

[8] T. S. Eliot, *Murder in the Cathedral* (New York: Harcourt Brace, 1935), 44.

ther that it was necessary for work and more profitable to be part of the Lutheran church. The young man later studied in London in the Reading Room of the British Museum and wrote, "Religion is the opiate of the people." Karl Marx was his name.

One bit of cynicism and hypocrisy can make a world of difference, and one Christian on his knees before God, with radical submission and a plea for mercy, changed by that prayer can change the world. Another man, Alexander Solzhenitsyn, in a prison camp in Siberia realized, "The line separating good and evil passes, not through states, nor between classes, nor between political parties either, but right through every human heart."

## A More Recent Illustration

Perhaps you remember the attempted revolution that was held in Tiananmen Square in China. If you do, I suspect the image burnt on your retina is that of one young man standing before a tank, shifting as it shifted, immovable. That is the kind of courage that is required to proclaim the mercy of the gospel of Jesus Christ as the solution to the problems of our world without the naivete that ignores the repressive structural evils. Or the hypocrisy that pretends that Christianity must not be lived as well as taught, that we who plead for mercy must have mercy. That sort of thoroughbred gospel commitment, undiluted, clear, fruitful, and brave, is the result of the heartfelt prayer of one broken, pious Israelite, on his knees before his master God asking for mercy.

## What We Need Is Mercy

Mercy for his captors? Mercy for his oppressors? Mercy for himself that he not give in to the sweet deceit of bitterness? Mercy eternally, that the suffering we wish to alleviate is not only the suffering in this world but even more the eternal suffering in the world to come. If it is unmerciful to give people the gospel without giving them bread, it is also unmerciful to give people bread and send them on their way with a full stomach to damnation, when we might alleviate that suffering through the proclamation of the gospel.

So we have rights, inhered to us by virtue of being made in the image of God, and we have responsibilities, the duties that Wolterstorff identifies as the reverse side of the same coin of those same rights. When the movie *Titanic* was being made, people were depicted scrambling and fighting to get into the life rafts, asserting themselves. What they did not show, for no one would have believed it, was the historical reality that the men let the women go first with the children, and many of them simply stood and watched and gave themselves to drown that others might be saved by their merciful sacrifice. As we think of justice, we need to go further and think of mercy and to ask for it and give it to those around us so that we can be vehicles for their receiving mercy too.

A SONG OF ASCENTS. OF DAVID.
If it had not been the LORD who was on our side—
	let Israel now say—
if it had not been the LORD who was on our side
	when people rose up against us,
then they would have swallowed us up alive,
	when their anger was kindled against us;
then the flood would have swept us away,
	the torrent would have gone over us;
then over us would have gone
	the raging waters.
Blessed be the LORD,
	who has not given us
	as prey to their teeth!
We have escaped like a bird
	from the snare of the fowlers;
the snare is broken,
	and we have escaped!
Our help is in the name of the LORD,
	who made heaven and earth.
—Psalm 124

# 5

# DANGER

In the cockpit of every commercial airliner there is a flight data recorder that runs on a thirty-minute loop taping the words of the pilot and crew as they talk to each other and to the control tower. The so-called black box is a prime piece of evidence when the causes of plane crashes are investigated. If you listen to the words of the pilot of US Airways Flight 1549 when it was forced to make an emergency landing in the Hudson River on January 15, 2009, you can hear remarkable calm, professionalism, and expertise in the face of extreme danger. In that particular case, all turned out well and it has been called "the most successful ditching in aviation history."[1]

All of us face danger on a daily basis. There are those of us who wonder where our next job is going to come from. There are others with physical challenges, or emotional ones. Some of us wonder where our next sermon is going to come from, or our next book. This psalm is the flight data recorder of the church facing danger. There are no expletives, no fear, no worries, no trauma, no panic, and no danger even in the face of danger. It was perhaps composed early in Israel's history as the nation was fighting for its very survival. The Philistines heard that David had been anointed king and so they sent their armies out not merely to threaten the newly established kingdom but to destroy it. David sought God's help, and the Israelites were victorious.

The church is always threatened by spiritual attacks and difficulties, but with the name of the Lord on our side danger need never become defeat. This psalm is telling us that God is the one who rescues us from danger. Psalm 120 starts with a call for help. Psalm 121 takes the step of

[1] Jeremy Olshan and Ikumulisa Livingston, "Quiet Air Hero Is Captain America," *New York Post*, January 17, 2009, http://www.nypost.com/seven/01172009/news/regionalnews/quiet_air_hero_is_captain_america_150593.htm. Accessed February 12, 2009.

looking up to God. Psalm 122 moves toward God's people. Psalm 123 asks God for mercy. Here, Psalm 124 rejoices that such help was found. This flight data recorder is a song of praise because the church's faith proved real, more real even than danger from people around. It is saying to us, "Sing this with me." When danger comes, God is the one who rescues. It makes two points about God's rescue from danger.

## When Danger Becomes Destruction

First, without God danger becomes destruction. We see this in verses 1 to 5:

> If it had not been the LORD who was on our side—
>     let Israel now say—
> if it had not been the LORD who was on our side
>     when people rose up against us,
> then they would have swallowed us up alive,
> when their anger was kindled against us;
>     then the flood would have swept us away,
> the torrent would have gone over us;
> then over us would have gone
>     the raging waters.

Danger can come in all shapes and sizes. The point of this first section is that this danger is *real*. It is real because it is from "people" (v. 2). There is an ongoing contrast in this psalm between man and the Lord. At the root of danger is the fear of man, and its antidote is the name of the Lord. People attack us, perhaps. People oppose us, perhaps. This danger is real. But it need not lead to defeat, because faith is even more real if the Lord is on our side.

This danger is not only real because it is from people; it is also real because it is fueled by real anger (v. 3). The church of God is often opposed because people are angry about what it stands for. Cain killed Abel. The Pharisees opposed Jesus. The Judaizers opposed Paul. There is a real opposition to Christians. It is from people. It is fueled by anger. But this danger is ultimately real because it is spiritual in nature. The psalmist uses metaphors in verses 3, 4, and 5 that indicate the spiritual nature of this battle. Our fight is not against flesh and blood. The danger that we face as Christians is of being "swallowed . . . up alive"

(v. 3), of a flood sweeping us away (v. 4), of being submersed by "raging waters" (v. 5). These are pictures of the forces of evil that oppose the work of God and which are, therefore, a very real danger.

How real it is for someone who does not know God! Perhaps you have some new danger in your life, and you are wondering why. Perhaps the answer is that what is found on the flight data recorder of your own life is intended to bring you to the place of asking for help from the Lord. Without God, danger becomes destruction. Don't let it. You're teetering on the edge, and God wants you to look at the reality of life. Faith is not a crutch. Faith is not for wimps. Muhammad Ali was taking a plane ride. The flight attendant asked him politely to put on his seat belt. He refused, saying, "Superman don't need no seat belt." The flight attendant replied, "Superman don't need no plane either." This reality of life that you are facing is a precursor to the ultimate reality of death, and who is going to rescue from that raging water? Man is but a breath, and all his devices are but a dream, but the name of the Lord stands forever. The name of the Lord is a strong tower; the righteous run into it and they are saved. You don't need a tower unless you have a battle.

So the danger is real, but rescue is too. God rescues from danger. First, without God danger becomes destruction *because the danger is real*. We're not playing here. This is life-and-death stuff. Without God, danger becomes destruction, but then also God rescues from danger.

## When Danger Becomes Witness

Second, with God danger becomes witness. We find this in the second half of the psalm in verses 6 to 8:

> Blessed be the LORD,
>     who has not given us
>     as prey to their teeth!
> We have escaped like a bird
>     from the snare of the fowlers;
> the snare is broken,
>     and we have escaped!
> Our help is in the name of the LORD,
>     who made heaven and earth.

Recently another Pakistani has been murdered for opposing the

Muslim blasphemy law in that country. Shabbhaz Bhatti was gunned down after leaving the home of his mother. Four months before his murder he recorded a video interview in which he not only predicted his death but explained why he would not back down despite the death threats. "I want to share that I believe in Jesus Christ," he had said, "who has given his own life for us. I know what is the meaning of the cross and I am following the cross."[2]

When we think of "witness," we tend to think of simplistic slogans or aggressive proselytism. But in Christian thought, the word *witness* is always connected to the expression of the cross as well as the experience of the cross. That's why the early Christians could sing in prison and why, when sent to jail for their witness, they brought out new converts with them. That is why Paul rejoiced in his sufferings, why the word for "witness" is the word for "martyr," and why this psalmist is so happy at his close escape from the jaws of death. He does not look back and say, "Why on earth did that happen?" He looks back and says, "Blessed be the Lord," and in so doing is a powerful witness.

There is no testimony like someone who has been close to the edge and come back again. In my experience that is not a one-off event but a pattern: God crushes us to reveal to us who he is in our weakness. I have to say, I look at this and think he sounds a bit too chirpy and chipper for my taste. He sounds a bit like the fake witness of someone who just says, "Praise the Lord! I'm really depressed." "Wonderful! Praise the Lord, I've got cancer!" "Great! Praise the Lord, I've just broken up with my girlfriend. Praise the Lord, I go back home to an empty house." "Praise the Lord! I have no idea who I am or what I'm meant to be doing."

But actually, he's still real here. The exclamation marks in the psalm may make it appear easy and breezy. But when you look carefully at the text, you can see that even as he witnesses now about what God has done for him, he does not hide how terrible it all has been. He was "prey to their teeth" (v. 6), being chewed up. He was in a "snare" (v. 7), like a bird caught in a hunter's trap. This was not pretty and perfect; it was bloody and ghastly.

---

[2] http://www.bbc.co.uk/news/world-south-asia-12644082.

But not anymore: God rescues us from danger. And as he does, danger becomes witness. I remember the remarkable experience of going to the family of a young man who had just fallen off a mountain in India, thousands of feet below. He had lain there strewn and broken and been rushed to the hospital. They did not know whether he would live or die at that point. I went with my pastoral tears ready to sit and weep with the family while they waited in the agony of being thousands of miles away from a loved one, and I found as I went in that they were gathered around together with a guitar, singing worship songs.

Such have Christians always been. Hymns in jail. Songs in the night. Blessed be the Lord as he rescues. Sometimes the rescue is healing or a miraculous new job the next day. But the real rescue is the change of heart, for without that, the new job or even the healing can lead to just yet more trouble. That young man was not healed. I visited him in the hospital when he came back to America. He was paraplegic. He had had countless well-meaning people come to pray for his healing. I prayed too, but I told him there might be a bigger healing plan that God had for him. Now he is a witness from his wheelchair—one of the most powerful I have ever met. I wonder if any postmodern secularist or Islamicist could present me with a man who has the power to embrace the cross like that.

With God, danger becomes witness. God rescues us from danger. Without God, danger becomes destruction. It rattles us. It shakes us. It exposes the foundations of our life. Use it as an opportunity to discover God again and to record on your flight data recorder a hymn of praise. You never know—it might be the most powerful thing you ever do.

## A Bigger Resonance

Of course, this psalm has an even bigger resonance. It points us to the cross and beyond to the resurrection. Surely Paul was thinking of this psalm and its meaning when he wrote, "What then shall we say to these things? *If God is for us, who can be against us?*" (Rom. 8:31). If the Lord had not been on our side—but he is. How do you know? He sent Jesus to die and rise again for his people. Put your trust in him and repent of your sins. The cross tells us that God has come to rescue us from our sin by taking the just judgment that we deserve in his own person that he might forgive, bearing that weight. If God is for us, and he is, who can be against us?

> *He who did not spare his own Son but gave him up for us all,* how will he not also with him graciously give us all things? [Good logic.] Who shall bring any charge against God's elect [his chosen people]? It is God who justifies [declares right]. Who is to condemn? Christ Jesus is the one who died—more than that, who was raised—who is at the right hand of God, who indeed is interceding for us. Who shall separate us from the love of Christ? Shall tribulation, or distress, or persecution, or famine, or nakedness, or danger, or sword? As it is written, "For your sake we are being killed all the day long; we are regarded as sheep to be slaughtered." No, in all these things we are more than conquerors through him who loved us. For I am sure that neither death nor life, nor angels nor rulers, nor things present nor things to come, nor powers, nor height nor depth, nor anything else in all creation, will be able to separate us from the love of God in Christ Jesus our Lord. (Rom. 8:31–39).

A Song of Ascents.
Those who trust in the Lord are like Mount Zion,
   which cannot be moved, but abides forever.
As the mountains surround Jerusalem,
   so the Lord surrounds his people,
   from this time forth and forevermore.
For the scepter of wickedness shall not rest
   on the land allotted to the righteous,
lest the righteous stretch out
   their hands to do wrong.
Do good, O Lord, to those who are good,
   and to those who are upright in their hearts!
But those who turn aside to their crooked ways
   the Lord will lead away with evildoers!
   Peace be upon Israel!
—Psalm 125

# 6

# SECURITY

All of us have insecurities. Whether because of our background and upbringing, our personality, or simply because of life experiences, there is not a person on the face of the planet who does not sometimes feel insecure. Beyond individual insecurities, though, there are also society-wide insecurities in the news from time to time: storms, earthquakes, aftershocks, and tsunamis; the whole Middle East and financial uncertainties. Throughout its history humanity has had reasons to feel insecure on occasion, though some say that recently there has been more than the average number of crises generating more than average insecurity. It feels especially hard at the moment to be grounded or secure. How do you find a sense of confidence, not blindly ignoring real danger, or covering up your private insecurities with overblown arrogance, but having confidence in the face of real insecurity?

## In the Real World

This psalm describes people who are secure in the real world. They "trust in the LORD" and so are "like Mount Zion, which cannot be moved, but abides forever" (v. 1) in the midst of real "wickedness" (v. 3). Still, it is easy to read those words and say to yourself, "That sounds good, but is it actually true?" Most probably read Psalm 125 and consign its message to pious platitudes for Sunday rather than to rugged teaching for business, politics, or personal life.

People want something more solid than being told to trust God, such as money or walls or armies. The Great Wall of China is thousands of miles long, 30 feet high, and 18 feet thick and was built as security against the northern invaders. It is a massive construction, visible from outer space, and was intended to be impenetrable. In fact, impressive as it was, the wall was breached not by physically breaking the wall down but by a simple ruse: the gatekeepers were bribed. A wall is only as strong as the people protecting it; an economy is only as strong as the people working in it; a business is only as strong as its staff; an army is only as strong as its soldiers. We can build walls to protect us, but walls are as strong (or as weak) as the humans that guard them. One bribe and the gates will open.

That is why this psalm tells us that our strength comes from whom we trust. "Those who trust in the LORD are like Mount Zion" (v. 1). Those people who trust God are so strong because their strength is not their own. They have resources beyond the human, beyond this life, in God himself. Those who trust in God are as strong as Mount Zion because, "as the mountains surround Jerusalem, so the LORD surrounds his people, from this time forth and forevermore" (v. 2).

This psalm is telling us that the way to find security is by trusting God. It gives us two reasons to trust God.

## God Protects

First, trust God because God protects.

> Those who trust in the LORD are like Mount Zion,
>      which cannot be moved, but abides forever.
> As the mountains surround Jerusalem,
>      so the LORD surrounds his people,
>      from this time forth and forevermore. (vv. 1–2)

Read those verses closely and you will see that they are intended to be pictured. "Those who trust in the LORD," he begins, "are *like* . . ." The Psalms are meant to help us fuse the rational and the emotional in our relationship with God, often by using picture language to restock our imagination. TV, videos, and films leave a visual residue in our mind. Let the pictures of this psalm fill the image gallery of your brain. "Those who trust in the LORD are *like* . . ." What are they like? They are "*like* Mount Zion, which cannot be moved, but abides forever." That is what people who trust in the Lord are like: Mount Zion, which cannot be moved but lasts forever.

What is God *like* to those people? "*As* the mountains surround Jerusalem, so the LORD surrounds his people, from this time forth and forevermore." Trust God because he protects like the mountains—solid, dependable, certain, secure—which surround Jerusalem. Those who trust him are *like Mount Zion*, which lasts forever.

You are in Jerusalem. You go up to Mount Zion. You stand there on the mountain, this famously strong citadel. Then you look up at the mountains surrounding you. You, if you trust God, are like that. Trusting God is not precarious. It is like being in the safest military stronghold that the author of this psalm could imagine. You are not walking on rotten boards on a half-sinking boat; you are patrolling the deck of your aircraft carrier.

Do not treat your faith, your trust, as something fragile like a flower that, if it is not constantly watered, will die. The psalm does not say that those who trust God are like fresh-cut flowers that last a few short weeks unless you have very green thumbs. Do not treat your faith as something vulnerable, like a person who is recovering from a disease will avoid all possible human contact to avoid infection. The psalm does not say that those who trust God are like someone with a weak immune system who might catch a spiritual cold at any moment. Treat your faith like a tank, like an aircraft carrier, like a fighter plane, like a department of defense with stockpiles of spiritual weapons, like a castle, like Mount Zion surrounded by mountains. Faith is not like a leap in the dark; it is like living in a stronghold.

### A Moving Picture

This picture is only really a snapshot of an ongoing movie. Mount Zion is mentioned for the first time here in these Psalms of Ascent, but from now on it occurs frequently. You can find Mount Zion mentioned in Psalms 126, 128, 129, 132, 133, and 134. Zion was the fortress mountain citadel that David first captured for the Israelites; later it came to refer to the whole of Jerusalem and in the New Testament to the heavenly Jerusalem, in the book of Hebrews and in Revelation.

So this psalm is not only just saying those who trust in the Lord are like a very firm, big mountain. Those people now equal God's people, whose story finishes with the city of God that lasts forever. This psalmist did not have the end of the story when he wrote. Neither do we, though we know more than he did. But the psalm is aware that the story will carry on; indeed it continues forever. These two verses are one freeze-frame in the whole story of God's people.

*A Picture to Put into Practice*

How do the picture of Mount Zion, the mountains of Jerusalem, and the story that continues throughout the New Testament of God's people, apply practically? As the psalmist sang this gospel song on the way up to Jerusalem, at times he felt insecure because of the dangers involved in ancient travel. As this song was sung by the workers who were rebuilding the walls of Jerusalem after the return from exile, they felt insecure because people threatened them to make them stop working. The picture of this psalm helped them when they put it into practice, and it will help you too when you put it into practice.

If you have ever been to a circus and watched a trapeze artist, you know that there is a pause between the flyer letting go and the catcher catching. As the flyer lets go, he has to hold himself absolutely still and wait, trusting that the catcher will catch him. He does not try to catch the catcher. He lets go, stays still, and waits to be caught. What enables that very real trust to take place? Practice. When a church building burns down, or a budget is not what we expected, or a family member acts in ways we wish he had not, as a Christian we are momentarily flying, if you like. We are in the gap, that pause between letting go—it seems—from all our securities and being caught by the catcher. What enables trust at that moment? "Faith comes from hearing, and hearing through the word of Christ" (Rom. 10:17). That gap between the flyer letting go and the catcher catching can be either the most terrifying, insecure place to be or the most exciting, exhilarating place to be, depending on what is going on in our mind, and that depends on what we have fed our mind, whether the insecurities of our culture or the certainties of God's Word. If it is the latter, the gap between letting go and being caught again is the simple joy of a child's being thrown in the air by an exuberant dad. There is a momentary surprise on her face as the child soars high and then bursts of delighted giggles as the child is caught again by her father. This picture of the first part of this psalm is intended to help us find security by trusting God through seeing that God protects. Trust God, the psalm is saying, first, because God protects.

## God Promises

Second, trust because God promises.

> For the scepter of wickedness shall not rest
>> on the land allotted to the righteous,
> lest the righteous stretch out
>> their hands to do wrong.
> Do good, O LORD, to those who are good,
>> and to those who are upright in their hearts!
> But those who turn aside to their crooked ways
>> the LORD will lead away with evildoers!
>> Peace be upon Israel! (vv. 3–5)

The second half of the psalm promises that God will do right, and that promise explains the confidence of the first half of the psalm. The word "For" at the beginning of verse 3 shows that the psalm is about to explain the previous verse. The promise itself then is that "the scepter of wickedness shall not rest on the land allotted to the righteous."

There are four results of this promise that are the basis for the confidence of the first half of the psalm. First, the righteous are confident to let God judge so that "the righteous [do not] stretch out their hands to do wrong." Second, the author of the psalm knows that God will protect those who trust him, so he can pray confidently, "Do good, O LORD, to those who are good, and to those who are upright in their hearts!" (Notice the biblical teaching of righteousness by faith, that those who "trust in the LORD" are the "upright in heart" who are "good.") Third, the author of the psalm realizes that such confidence comes not on his own merits but from God, so he is wary of turning away from God: "Those who turn aside to their crooked ways the LORD will lead away with evildoers!" Fourth, on the basis of this promise, God's people are confidently urged to be at peace: "Peace be upon Israel!"

The story goes that in the 1960s a man decided to re-preach Jonathan Edwards's famous sermon, "Sinners in the Hands of an Angry

God." However, the preacher modified the sermon to better fit with the era. He entitled the sermon, "Seekers Who Lack Self-Esteem in the Hands of a Full-Esteem God." In the original, Edwards preached to those who did not trust God: "You have offended him infinitely more than ever a stubborn rebel did his prince; and yet it is nothing but his hand that holds you from falling into the fire every moment." Edwards described those who do not trust God as being like a spider hanging by a thread over a pit. Such preaching has always offended some and been misunderstood by others. It is said that the 1960s preacher decided that the spider analogy was too strong medicine for modern people and switched it to a butterfly: "Somewhere in the forest a butterfly was beautifying a rose by posing atop its petals. Her wings flapping to an unheard tune the trees seemed to be swaying to. A bee was humming to the melody of nature's symphony as he dipped inside a wonderfully painted forest flower that seemed delighted to have such a distinguished visitor. Bluebirds were singing, crickets chirping and a possum was laughing in the gentle breeze. Heaven seemed to be saying, 'You're the most important creature in the woodlands . . . yes, you . . . and you . . . and you with the compound eyes.'"

Few preachers would actually drown their congregation in such sentimentality, but who would be as brave as Edwards? More to the point, who would preach the first part of verse 5 of Psalm 125?

> But those who turn aside to their crooked ways
> the LORD will lead away with evildoers!

Yet preaching that, and believing it, is a part of trusting God too. Those who trust him God will keep secure. Those who "turn aside to their crooked ways" (the opposite of trusting God), God "will lead away with evildoers." Here is how you know whether you are trusting God: is your life, in the midst of the storm, like Mount Zion, solid and immovable, or are you shaken by every whisper of breeze, fearing it is the premonition of the end and the storm that is to come? The scepter of the wicked may rule for a while over the land allotted to the righteous, but not for long. So those who trust God secure themselves with the thought that the end is coming. They do not take the law into their own hands; rather, they trust God with his final vindication. Immovable are they. Resolute are they. Dependable. Firm. Secure. Like a rock. Like a mountain, with storms of rain lashing against it.

Not so the wicked. They are:

> like chaff that the wind drives away.
> Therefore the wicked will not stand in the judgment,
>     nor sinners in the congregation of the righteous;
> for the Lord knows the way of the righteous,
>     but the way of the wicked will perish. (Ps. 1:4–6)

Instead:

> Kiss the Son,
>     lest he be angry, and you perish in the way,
>     for his wrath is quickly kindled.
> Blessed are all who take refuge in him. (Ps. 2:12)

Those who trust God cannot be moved. Those who trust in him are unshakable, unflappable, immovable, strong, and resolute, because even when the buildings shake all around them they are building their lives upon an unshakable foundation, upon God himself.

That is why so many people today are drifting—they lack that foundation.

Not so the righteous. They trust in God. They are like Mount Zion. The Lord surrounds them. They are secure. They are at peace. May that be so for you today.

A Song of Ascents.
When the Lord restored the fortunes of Zion,
    we were like those who dream.
Then our mouth was filled with laughter,
    and our tongue with shouts of joy;
then they said among the nations,
    "The Lord has done great things for them."
The Lord has done great things for us;
    we are glad.
Restore our fortunes, O Lord,
    like streams in the Negeb!
Those who sow in tears
    shall reap with shouts of joy!
He who goes out weeping,
    bearing the seed for sowing,
shall come home with shouts of joy,
    bringing his sheaves with him.
—Psalm 126

# 7

# LAUGHTER

Spurgeon was once criticized for putting too much laughter into his sermons. Frivolous. Lacking gravity. His reply to the woman who had buttonholed him was classic: "My good lady, if you only knew how much I restrain myself." This psalm shows us not only that "laughter" (v. 2) and God go together but also God and "joy" (vv. 2, 5, and 6). This psalm is written to help you discover the secret of joy.

## Mistaken Notions of Joy

When the psalm refers to joy, it does not mean the tendency that some people have, because of their temperament, to be happier than other people. For one reason or another there appear to be people who are more naturally wired to smile, who can wake up in the morning singing a cheery song, and who look at their breakfast cereal and simply clap their hands with delight. You may feel sympathy with the Snoopy T-shirt that was popular when Charlie Brown was all the rage—"I hate people who sing in the morning"—but then others get up early because they like it. Some people are morning people, some people are evening people, and some people seem to feel happier than others. They are wired that way. However, the joy here is not this matter of temperament.

Nor is this joy about faking it, the sort of pretend joy that plasters a smile on your face while inside you growl. Nor is it imposing joy on others by going up to someone who that moment discovered his best friend had a car accident and telling him to "rejoice in the Lord always," to which the understandable reply might be, "Let me punch you in the nose and see how much rejoicing you're doing then." Nor is it the deep Christian joy that is so deep—soooo deep—that to find it you practically have to set up an oil well. Drilling, drilling, deeper,

deeper, deeper. Ah, we have struck oil; there is a smile down there; it was *deep* Christian joy.

## Living the Dream

No, this joy is not a matter of temperament (your natural predisposition), an experience that must be manufactured for yourself and other people (faking it), or something so deep that it is not really happy (where the smile goes down rather than up). Instead, this joy is a result of being "restored" by God (v. 1)—not happy because of your genetics but happy because of what God has done for you. This joy is based upon an objective, real, God-given restoration. And those who have this joy are "like those who dream" (v. 1). The ancient world, when it referred to dreams, did not, first of all, mean a daydream. They meant an actual dream, the sort of dream you have when you are asleep. So when the psalmist says this was like dreaming, he is comparing joy to a very good actual dream. He is saying that this joy is like *that*. This joy is so good that when you experience it you think, "I am living the dream." Such is the joy that this psalm is talking about.

So throw away all ideas that joy is found in things apart from God, or that God is the serious, gloomy, despondent, negative, critical sort of religious freak who will smack you over the wrists with a wooden ruler as soon as you step out of line. This psalm, first, describes the dream and then, second, tells you how that dream comes true.

## The Dream

First, the dream:

> When the LORD restored the fortunes of Zion,
>     we were like those who dream.
> Then our mouth was filled with laughter,
>     and our tongue with shouts of joy;
> then they said among the nations,
>     "The LORD has done great things for them."
> The LORD has done great things for us;
>     we are glad. (vv. 1–3)

Zion, as the last chapter explained, stands for the whole story of the people of God that finishes in the heavenly Jerusalem—"When the

Lord restored the fortunes of Zion," that is, when God brought back hss people to where they should have been all along. Notice there is a parallel between verse 1 and verse 4. Verse 1 says, "When the Lord restored" or "When God restored." Verse 4 prays, "Restore our fortunes, O Lord" or "Please, God, restore." So the first part of the psalm is the dream, what happened when God restored. The second part of the psalm is how to live the dream, asking God to restore your fortunes.

## Being Restored

"Fortune" here doesn't mean luck or chance. It is not saying, "I've been playing the gaming tables and finally I got lucky." It is not saying, "I've been down on my luck and finally I got my lucky break." The word "fortune" here mirrors the word "restore," so "When the Lord restored the fortunes of Zion" (v. 1) means something like "When God *restored* us to a *restored* situation." We find the same in verse 4, which is parallel: "Restore our fortunes, O Lord," meaning, "*Restore* us to this *restored* situation, O Lord." This matters because people think they are "living the dream" when they have bought a new vacation home or a whole new wardrobe from Savile Row. Truly such people are missing real joy. Joy is not financially living well or looking good. Joy is about being *restored*, that is, brought back to who you were designed to be.

## Laughter

If joy is being restored, what is being restored like? "We were like those who dream." What sort of dream? Now the dream is described: "Then our mouth was filled with laughter" (v. 2). See the laughter clearly in your mind. This laughter is not a little tweak of the lips. This is not a polite living-room chortle. This is not a snigger behind your hand. This is not a mild happy laugh. This is a slap-your-thigh, burst-out-in-laughter, LOL, giggle fit. "Our mouth was filled with laughter"—wide open, yawning chasm, filled with laughter.

Wide-mouthed laughter is how the psalm describes the dream. This is not one of those church-bulletin blooper jokes you can find online. You know, "The epistles are wives of the apostles," "The fifth commandment is humor thy father and mother," "Lot's wife was a pillar of salt by day but a ball of fire by night," "Noah's wife was Joan of Ark," and the rest. This is tears rolling down your face, laughing out loud, together—not just "my own" but God's people together—engaged in wide-open-mouthed laughter. This joy makes you laugh so hard that there is no room for anything else in your mouth!

### Shouts

"And our tongue [was filled] with shouts of joy" (v. 2). Other versions translate this "songs" (not shouts) of joy, but if it is singing, it is the volume you hear that lifts the roof at a sports stadium. This is the fist-pump shout when you score a touchdown, or hit a home run, or score straight As on your tests.

### Witness

There is still more to this description of the dream: "Then they said among the nations, 'The LORD has done great things for them'" (v. 2). When they started laughing out loud, really loud, and shouting songs of joy, then everyone around looked at them and thought, "Whoa, something good's going on there. I want to be a part of that!" The people of God agreed with this verdict: "The LORD has done great things for us; we are glad" (v. 3).

I do not think there is any type of person who, if they truly understand this psalm, would not want the dream it describes. Whatever your temperament (morning person or not), whatever your situation (tough or easy), do you not desire to have a constant joy that is so amazing and so obvious that people all around you say, "I want some of that joy juice he's on"? The dream is described as God's restoring his people, which causes laughter, joy, and witness.

## The Dream Come True

Second, the dream come true:

> Restore our fortunes, O LORD,
>      like streams in the Negeb!
> Those who sow in tears
>      shall reap with shouts of joy!
> He who goes out weeping,

bearing the seed for sowing,
shall come home with shouts of joy,
bringing his sheaves with him. (vv. 4–6)

Verses 4 to 6 develop a model of praying for the dream to come true and a contrast of what it is like when that dream does come true. To begin with, "Restore our fortunes, O LORD" (v. 4) mirrors the description that runs from verses 1 to 3 of fortunes restored. Having described that dream in the first half of the psalm, now in the second half the psalm begins to model the surprising contrast of being restored. Being restored is a contrast "like streams in the Negeb" (v. 4), Negeb meaning "parched" or "dry," the southern part of the country. So "like streams in the Negeb" contrasts water with a desert. We find another contrast: "Those who sow in tears shall reap with shouts of joy! He who goes out weeping, bearing the seed for sowing, shall come home with shouts of joy, bringing his sheaves with him" (vv. 5–6). So tears contrast with shouts of joy. Verses 4 to 6, then, model asking God to restore his people. They tell us that God's restoration contrasts water flowing in a desert and shouting with joy after crying. Let me explain this model and contrast of joy with the mnemonic H-A-P-P-Y.

H—humility. Joy begins with humility. To say, "Restore, O LORD," requires the humility to admit that you need restoring. Jesus said, "Blessed [or happy] are the poor in spirit, for theirs is the kingdom of heaven. Blessed are those who mourn, for they shall be comforted. Blessed are the meek, for they shall inherit the earth. Blessed are those who hunger and thirst for righteousness, for they shall be satisfied" (Matt. 5:3–6). This psalm is saying that restoration begins with having the humility to ask for it.

A—advice. Notice it is "our" (v. 4), not "my," fortunes. The psalmist is doing this in community. Let me make a pastoral sidebar here. There is a medical condition called "clinical depression." I have known people, very godly, holy people, who are clinically depressed. This is not because they are sinning. It is not because they are not praying enough or trying hard enough. It is because there is a medical condition called "clinical depression." If you have felt sad for a long time, and you talk to someone who cares about you and knows you well and they say,

"Well, maybe you should go and see someone," then just do it. You have nothing to lose other than your pride. That is different from being temperamentally slightly melancholic or Eeyore-like. That's a personality type, a glass-half-empty kind of person. Fine. But if it's more than that, get some advice.

P—perspective. There is a perspective going on in this contrast. Negeb, streams flowing in the desert. Tears, leading to joy. So far in these Psalms of Ascent we have been through the dark side of the emotions, asking for help; now we are coming to the bright side of the emotions: joy, happiness, in God. The perspective here is the story line of the Bible. What we are really talking about is the gospel. So this is not merely a contrast of a cathartic effect—weeping then rejoicing. This is saying, "Because of who God is, because of what the gospel is, if you turn to God he will restore you."

The story of the gospel is that God has come to rescue us in Christ. Part of experiencing true joy is keeping that perspective your perspective. It's working hard at whatever is noble and true and thinking about such things (see Phil. 4:8). The point of Paul's words there in Philippians is not just looking at a flower rather than at a depressing piece of news, though that can be wise at times. It is looking at the flower and asking, "What does that tell me about who God is as the creator?" It is asking, when you hear that bit of bad news, "What does that tell me about the fallen world, and how glad does that make me that God is going to make a new heaven and a new earth, and he is redeeming his people through the gospel?" Perspective, perspective. Martyn Lloyd-Jones in his book *Spiritual Depression* says, "The trouble with Christians is they listen to themselves when they should talk to themselves."[1] Talk to yourself, that is, in the sense of adopting a gospel perspective of what is happening.

P—prayer. This is a prayer: "Restore our fortunes, O LORD." Some of us need to slow down to make room for prayer. Let me ask you a direct question: are you having a regular, daily quiet time? I don't mean with four other people in the room in a Bible study, good as that is; or

[1] D. Martyn Lloyd-Jones, *Spiritual Depression: Its Causes and Cure* (Grand Rapids, MI: Eerdmans, 1965), 20–21.

with your family in devotions, excellent as that is. I mean you on your knees or in your favorite chair, with the Bible open, quiet around, and connecting with God in prayer and saying, "Lord, would you restore me to joy?"

Y—you. I wrote a book called *The God Centered Life*, so why am I now talking about *you*?[2] I am, because to be truly joyful, you need to be restored to who you were designed to be. It is *restoration*, coming back to the way you were meant to be as designed by God. It is a God-centered you. The gospel enables you to become *you* as you were meant to be, the new creation. It is to be reconciled to God, to be in Christ and Christ in you, to have your sins removed and his righteousness yours as you are in Christ. This restoration happens as you become a Christian; it happens more and more as you follow Christ.

Sherlock Holmes and Dr. Watson were out camping. Holmes woke up Watson in the middle of the night and pointed up at the stars. Watson blinked the sleep out of his eyes as Holmes asked what he deduced. Watson said, "Well, astronomically, I deduce there are millions of galaxies and potentially billions of planets. Astrologically, I deduce that Saturn is in Leo. Horologically, I deduce that the time is approximately a quarter past three. Meteorologically, I deduce that we will have a beautiful day tomorrow. What about you, Holmes," he said, "what do you deduce?" "Watson," said Holmes slowly, "I deduce that someone has stolen our tent."

Joy is both very complex and very simple. I studied the Puritans at Cambridge University. My teacher was a senior, eminent professor toward the end of his career, a brilliant man. I remember talking to him once about the caricature of Puritans as a dour and despondent lot, the puritanical myth. He said to me, "Whenever you meet a Puritan [he used the present tense *meet*, for he knew that there are still Puritans today, even if they wear jeans and have tattoos instead of wide-brimmed hats and buckled shoes], you meet a happy person."

We tend to think that being happy is being trite, and the more miserable we are, the more profound we must be. Nothing could be

---

[2] Josh Moody, *The God-Centered Life: Insights from Jonathan Edwards for Today* (Vancouver: Regent, 2007).

further from the truth. God's ultimate destiny for us who will believe is not miserable profundity but joyful severity, a thrill that reverberates with the truth that "God himself will be with them as their God. He will wipe away every tear from their eyes, and death shall be no more, neither shall there be mourning, nor crying, nor pain anymore, for the former things have passed away" (Rev. 21:3–4). For those who will put their trust in God that is their destiny, and it is one filled with joy.

A Song of Ascents. Of Solomon.
Unless the Lord builds the house,
    those who build it labor in vain.
Unless the Lord watches over the city,
    the watchman stays awake in vain.
It is in vain that you rise up early
    and go late to rest,
eating the bread of anxious toil;
    for he gives to his beloved sleep.
Behold, children are a heritage from the Lord,
    the fruit of the womb a reward.
Like arrows in the hand of a warrior
    are the children of one's youth.
Blessed is the man
    who fills his quiver with them!
He shall not be put to shame
    when he speaks with his enemies in the gate.
—Psalm 127

# 8

# BEATING THE DAILY GRIND

Why is it that many of us spend our lives doing things that, if we are really honest, looking in the mirror late at night, we do not enjoy? "The daily grind." "Nine to five." "Another day, another dollar." Why is it that some people study so hard to have this kind of work—a BA, an MA, a PhD—only to discover that they still have no JOB? And then when you consider working life in this way, you naturally wonder whether instead family life is where you can expect fulfillment. And if that is the case, why is it that one of the best-selling books on family life is called *Families and How to Survive Them*, not *Families and How to Make Them Even Happier*? Are families really more like fudge, mostly sweet but with a few nuts, something you simply have to accept whereas you can choose your friends?

## The Goal of the Psalm

This psalm is talking about the daily grind, or life lived "in vain" as it puts it, at work (vv. 1–2) and in family (vv. 3–5). The goal of the psalm is to show us how to see both family and work from God's perspective so that the daily grind is beaten.

The psalm, then, talks about watching (v. 1) and beholding (v. 3) to encourage a certain perspective on normal, everyday life. It wants you to *look* this way at houses, whether the house you are literally building or the household of your family. It wants you to look this way at the city, watchman watching over the city (defense may be included, watchman on the lookout to give the alarm when cities are threatened). This daily life of work and family can be a frustration; it can be little more than a daily grind, but with the perspective of this psalm there is opportunity to no longer live "in vain." Whether that frustration you feel is a difficult boss or an intransigent staff, an inflexible parent or a rebellious teenager, the lack of work or too much work, looking at life the way the psalm suggests will change your experience of life. It will give a new perspective on the troubled teenager whose actions help his parents have sympathy with animals who eat their young. It will give a new perspective on growing up in a family where every emotion was buried six feet under the ground. It will give a new perspective on factory work, making payroll, or policing a city.

So this psalm is not about hymns and songs and organs and guitars and church, as good as those things are. It is not about Sunday worship and putting on your Sunday best. It is builders building. Laborers laboring. Guards guarding. Rising "early" and working "late" (v. 2), what we call "burning the candle at both ends." It is about couples with young children not being able to remember when they last had a whole night's sleep. Farmers working from dawn to dusk to bring in the harvest. Shift workers with two jobs. The stuff of life, the daily grind. How do you beat it? You beat it by adopting the perspective of the psalm.

## The Importance of Perspective

You may say the way you look at things does not change the way they are, but your perspective does change how you feel about those things and the attitude you bring to them. And that changes the way you live. So think of your favorite painting. Perhaps a classic Constable of the rolling English countryside that makes you yearn for clotted cream, green fields, and a proper English pub with proper English beer. Or a Winslow Homer of the sailboat where you can almost smell the New England clam chowder. As you think of your favorite painting, you will realize that the way it encourages you to see life influences how you look at life, and that can influence how you live life. That is the power of Salvador Dalí's melting clocks, or Hopper's "Nighthawks" with its atmosphere of ennui, boredom, and emptiness late at night. Or a Caravaggio. These pictures do not just look nice; they are not merely aesthetic in the sense of "Oh, that's pretty." They are intended to tell us something about how we look at life or how the artist looks at life. That is the power of a film too: it can encourage us to look at life a certain way, and that can change how we live life. Such pictures have great potential for good, or harm, depending on the perspective they encourage and whether or not we adopt that perspective.

This psalm is painting a picture of reality, and it is asking you to watch and behold life like that. Seeing life as it were through the eyes of God, that is, with his perspective, is the way not to live in vain. (The word for "vain" here is not the same as the word for "vanity" in the book of Ecclesiastes, though the concept is similar. How then do you beat the daily grind?

## Seeing Work as God Does

First, beat the daily grind by seeing work as God does:

> Unless the LORD builds the house,
>     those who build it labor in vain.
> Unless the LORD watches over the city,
>     the watchman stays awake in vain.
> It is in vain that you rise up early
>     and go late to rest,
> eating the bread of anxious toil;
>     for he gives to his beloved sleep. (vv. 1–2)

The perspective on work that the psalm is encouraging you to adopt is a conditional perspective. The first two verses have a conditional clause hardwired into their structure: unless *this* takes place *that* will never happen. "*Unless* the LORD builds the house" (v. 1)—"unless" introduces the conditional clause. Most people know there is a conditional clause to effective work, but that conditional clause is very different from this one. Most people think that effective work is conditional upon their activity, not upon God's activity. They think, "If I come up with a good human technique at my workplace, if I do A, B, and C, if I follow all the rules, *then* I will flourish." But this psalm is saying that even for practical daily work, the nine to five, the conditional clause is not human building but God building. "*Unless* the LORD builds the house, those who build it labor in vain," not "Unless I get the perfect human technique, I'll be laboring in vain."

"Unless the LORD builds the house" is what in Aristotelian philosophy would be called a primary cause (God building) and then a secondary cause (you working). The psalm is, of course, not saying,

"Don't work," or that clever ideas and human effort are unimportant. It is saying that even the best technique and even the hardest work will be entirely frustrated, "in vain," unless the primary cause, God building, is occurring. "*Unless* the LORD builds the house, those who build it labor in vain"—that is, if God is not the cause of this building, however much they labor it is in vain. This primary cause is necessary for the secondary cause, we working, to have any impact.

*The Condition Illustrated*

Verse 1 illustrates this conditional perspective—"*Unless* the LORD . . ."—in two ways: by building and watching over the city. Each time, it is introduced by the same phrase, "Unless the LORD . . .": for building, "*Unless the* LORD builds the house, those who build it labor in vain"; for watching, "*Unless the* LORD watches over the city, the watchman stays awake in vain." The conditional perspective is true then for building as well as for watching over the city.

Verse 2 shows what it is like not to live with this perspective and then what it is like to live with this perspective. Hard work is there either way but not pointless work. "It is in vain that you rise up early and go late to rest" (v. 2) is not saying "Do not work so hard," but the hard work you are doing will be frustrating unless the condition of depending on God is met. The psalm tells you there is no point working hard unless you are depending upon God, not that there is no point working hard at all. Not only ineffectiveness but also worry is the result of not living according to the perspective of depending upon God. "Unless the LORD . . . ," you will only be "eating the bread of anxious toil" (v. 2). That worry, that vanity, the daily grind, is the human condition unless you are one of his "beloved" (v. 2).

The word "beloved" could be a sort of hidden signature of Solomon. We are told in the inscription of the psalm that it was written by Solomon. And Solomon's special name, given to him by God, was Jedidiah (2 Sam. 12:25), which means "beloved of the LORD." So the psalm is saying that you need to be one of God's beloved for work to be effective, whether the work is building buildings, watching over cities, or even high-end government executive responsibilities like those of King Solomon. If we are his beloved, then all of this will not be in vain. We will beat the daily grind.

There is a story of a preacher and his wife visiting the Caribbean—beautiful place, beautiful beaches, beautiful sea, beautiful weather. They were asked to dine with one of the wealthiest men in the world, who had a massive mansion there. This man was seventy-five years old, and throughout the whole meal he was crying or at least at the point of weeping. He said to the visiting preacher and his wife, "I am the most miserable man in the world. Out there is my yacht. I can go anywhere I want. I have my private plane, my helicopters. I have everything I want to make my life happy, yet I am as miserable as hell." Of course the preacher and his wife attempted to share Christ, through whom we become one of God's beloved as we put our faith in him. Later the same day this same preacher and his wife went to visit the pastor of a local Baptist church. This man was also seventy-five years old, a widower who spent most of his time looking after and taking care of his two invalid sisters. This pastor said to the visiting preacher and his wife, "I don't have two dollars to my name, but I am the happiest man on this island." The visiting preacher was Billy Graham and his wife was Ruth, and as he recounted the story after they left, Billy turned to Ruth and said, "Who do you think is the richer man?" It is a question that answers itself. And yet people try to build buildings and watch over cities without taking God into account, and in the end it will all turn to ashes in their mouths unless they are one of his beloved.

## Being Beloved

How much did this psalm ring hollow for Solomon toward the end of his life? How much did he listen to the advice that he had written here and how much did he obey it? We do not know. But it is written for us to realize that to flourish in life, you must be in the center of God's love; that is, put your trust in Jesus and walk by the Spirit and look at life that way. Follow him morally, spiritually, with Bible open, in prayerful dependence upon God, praying that God would bless your work nine to five—your business deals, your scholarship and art—doing all for Jesus, for we know that he loves us. That is how you beat the daily grind at work. Your work becomes a love, a love for God, who has given you this opportunity to love him back. As Paul says, you do it "as for the Lord" (Col. 3:23), not as for men, but as for the Master. Everything is transformed by this perspective of being loved by God.

## Seeing Family as God Does

Second, beat the daily grind by seeing family as God does:

> Behold, children are a heritage from the LORD,
>     the fruit of the womb a reward.
> Like arrows in the hand of a warrior
>     are the children of one's youth.
> Blessed is the man
>     who fills his quiver with them!
> He shall not be put to shame
>     when he speaks with his enemies in the gate. (vv. 3–5)

In the second part of the psalm (vv. 3–5) the psalmist uses similar language to the first part (vv. 1–2) to connect the two points about work and the family to the overall theme. Building a house, the first part, is now building the household of your family, the second part. The word for "behold" is frequently used in biblical language, but here I think it is particularly encouraging us specifically to see in a certain way. The word "behold" emphasizes the theme of *perspective*, the overall theme of how you look at life that began with watching in the first part of the psalm and now continues to beholding in the second part of the psalm.

So from verse 3 to the end of the psalm, you are encouraged to look at children, to behold children, as God does. Children are a "heritage from the LORD" (v. 3), "like arrows in the hand of a warrior" (v. 4), that which makes a man "blessed" (v. 5). Now, lots of people will say that children are a wonderful blessing, but in practice sometimes you wonder if the saying that "grandchildren are God's reward for not killing your own children" has some truth to it. The blessing of children can look clearer in retrospect, or rosier in prospect, than does the daily reality when children are the dominating aspect of your life. But this psalm is not putting on rose-tinted spectacles when it looks at children and saying how wonderful it was to change four diapers at three in the morning for two years. It is not pious platitude. It is real life in the trenches with family, whether youngsters, teenagers, or adult children. It presents three unusual shifts of perspective.

### Children as Heritage

First, children are your heritage. "Behold, children are a heritage from the LORD" (v. 3). This "behold" is carrying on the theme of perspective and saying, "Look at children as your inheritance from God." Now, look carefully at how it describes children: "Behold, children are a *heritage* from the LORD." It does not say, "Children inherit from you," (though that is normally true), but that children are your inheritance from God, if you are a parent. That is an unfamiliar way of looking at children. It is a shift of perspective about family. I want you to hold on to that shift of perspective, because each of these shifts of perspective is like a piece of a jigsaw puzzle picture.

### Children as Reward

Second, children are your reward. The next puzzle piece of this perspective on children is "the fruit of the womb a reward" (v. 3). This does not mean that children are our reward for being morally good. No, the theology that God through his grace gives us everything and that we deserve nothing is assumed here. It is not talking about moral rewards. This is saying that, in one sense, children are going to be *our* reward. The word for reward here does mean simply "reward"; it also means "hire" and "payment." It is a money word. It is the same word that Jonah uses when he pays to hire a boat (Jonah 1:3). So this reward is not about the fact that all is by grace and is an undeserved blessing from God. That is assumed. We often think, understandably enough, that children are going to cost us a lot of money, but this is saying that we actually need to switch perspective. They reward us. Hold onto that piece of this jigsaw puzzle picture.

### Children as Weapons

Third, children are your weapon. "Like arrows in the hand of a warrior are the children of one's youth" (v. 4). Many Christians are so familiar with this part of the Bible that you can forget what a strange idea this is. Could anything be further from the natural thought of a new dad?

"How's it going with your newborn baby?"

"Oh, it's like arrows in my hand. I feel like going out on the gun range and shooting some targets. I feel so lithe. I've got so much energy."

Yet, "blessed is the man who fills his quiver" with these arrows. A quiver is where you put your arrows. It is like a bullet belt for a gun. It is a strange idea that each child is another bullet to put in your belt. "He shall not be put to shame when he speaks with his enemies in the gate" (v. 5).

### Motivation to Have Children

In one sense, what this is saying is obvious. It is simply saying that children are a good thing. But it is trying to help us see *why* that is the case even when we do not feel as if it is true. It is giving us a surprising shift of perspective. It is saying, "Children do not inherit; parents inherit." It is saying, "Children do not get rewarded; parents get rewarded." It is saying, "Children do not make us weak, old, and exhausted; they make us ready for battle." Together the puzzle pieces create a picture of children as your reward, your inheritance, and your arrows, because when you are older, having strong, godly children around you will protect you.

I want you to notice that this motivating language toward having children speaks to male sensibilities. I know there are women who do not really want children. I know there are men who long for children. But here is distinctly male motivation for the man who wants the wife but is not sure about the children: great inheritance, great pay, and really good at winning battles. All this means "he shall not be put to shame when he speaks with his enemies in the gate." The gate was the place either of battle where a city was defended against those who were trying to sack it or where law courts met to administer justice and settle disputes. In either scenario, facing battle or facing a lawsuit, a man who has strong sons around him will be well protected. He will have children to fight with him when there is war and children to speak up for him when there is a dispute.

Certainly, even believing that children are great does not stop them from being a strain at times. Someone said to me that you spend the first few years of your children's lives teaching them to walk and talk, and then the next dozen years of your children's lives training them to sit and be quiet. Perhaps children can exhaust even the most devoted parents to such an extent as to take literally the advice on the aspirin bottle: "Take two aspirin and *keep away from children*." But in the perspective of this psalm, it is astonishing that many in the developed world are reconsidering their historic commitment to have more children than the number of parents. Assuredly, in some parts of the world, population growth still worries environmentalists and those who plan to make sure there are enough resources for everyone. But Western society, at least in parts of Europe, is having fewer children than the previous generation. This means their future is drying up, for in the view of this psalm, children, expensive as they may be at the front end, are an investment in our future.

*Spiritual Children*

If you are not married or if you cannot have children, this does not mean that God is not blessing you. There are many examples in the Bible of the spiritual children that you can have. Paul, for instance, was a father figure for Timothy. When you tell someone the gospel, you may have the privilege of seeing a new birth, and that can be just as much, even more, of a blessing. You can invest in pastoral and discipleship work, ministry as heritage from God. Many people have done that. But whether physical or spiritual or both, I rather like the remark from the commentator Derek Kidner on this passage: "The greater their promise, the more likely it is that these sons will be a handful before they are a quiverful."[1]

## Looking at Life Differently Because of This Psalm

How, then, do we look at life differently? We have to have correct theological assumptions. There *is* vanity—life in vain, the daily grind—

[1] Derek Kidner, *Psalms 73–150*, Tyndale Old Testament Commentaries (Downers Grove, IL: IVP Academic, 1975), 442.

because there is something broken about life. We have to be honest about that. Otherwise, we will develop a false hope that heaven can be created on earth. Heaven is not here; here is vanity. That said, though, there is also a perspective that beats the daily grind. It is not by the escapism of shopping therapy, watching movies, or working hard enough to numb yourself but by a switch of perspective to bring God back into view in everyday life—family and work. See life through God's eyes, work dependent upon God, and children as a blessing from God, and you will beat the daily grind.

### See beyond the Mundane

Perhaps one of the most controversial and well-known forms of modern art is street art, not simply graffiti but the higher-end street art of people like the incognito Banksy. All art, controversial or not—pictures and paintings—asks us to look at life in a certain way. Similarly, this psalm asks us to watch and behold beyond the mundane. What if commuting to the office in one small box to work in another bigger box, the daily grind, can be beaten? What if vanity, vanity, vanity (three times repeated in this psalm) can be transcended by the man who is blessed by God? What if you beat the daily grind by seeing that life—work and family—is vanity "*unless* the LORD builds the house"? In other words, what if this psalm speaks truly? The only way you are going to find out is by putting it into practice. Next time you feel your daily life is a daily grind, change your perspective.

A Song of Ascents.
Blessed is everyone who fears the Lord,
    who walks in his ways!
You shall eat the fruit of the labor of your hands;
    you shall be blessed, and it shall be well with you.
Your wife will be like a fruitful vine
    within your house;
your children will be like olive shoots
    around your table.
Behold, thus shall the man be blessed
    who fears the Lord.
The Lord bless you from Zion!
    May you see the prosperity of Jerusalem
    all the days of your life!
May you see your children's children!
    Peace be upon Israel!
—Psalm 128

# 9

# THE BLESSING OF FAMILY

In the cartoon *Calvin and Hobbes*, the loveable rogue Calvin goes on a disastrous family holiday. His father's dream was to camp in the middle of nowhere and experience nature. It rained. It rained every single day nonstop. It rained when they cooked. It rained when they went fishing. It rained when they tried to start a fire. Calvin's father kept on smiling. He tried desperately to cheer up everyone else in the family. But in the end even his enthusiasm was washed away by the rain. He gave in, packed to leave early, shouting in frustration above the noise of the thunder. And the moment everything had been put away ready to go, the rain stopped and the sun came out.

Family life can have its ironies, but this psalm presents such an idyllic family life that it might feel to some as if it stretches credibility. It is all "blessing" (vv. 1, 2, 4, 5), "fruit" (vv. 2, 3), "prosperity" (v. 5), and "peace" (v. 6). The author of this psalm has obviously never watched an *Oprah* show, or read a *Calvin and Hobbes* cartoon. You even wonder too whether he has read the Bible, for the story of Abraham and Sarah, or David and his wives, hardly lives up to this sales job of families who fear the Lord. One way to understand what this psalm is actually saying is by the ancient church's motto *fides et sacramentum*. The idea was that in marriage and family there is a blessing to believe (*fides*) and a blessing to receive (*sacramentum*). That ancient summary of the Bible's teaching about the sanctity of marriage and family was formulated in response to the pagan world's more fluid and less stable concept of marriage. Similarly this (much older) psalm is not pretending that God-fearing families are perfect, but it is advocating for their blessing. It is not saying, "Family life is always wonderful if you say your prayers," or, "Every Christian household is always happy." Instead, the psalm is saying, first, "Believe the blessing of fearing the Lord," and then, second, "Receive this blessing."

## Believe the Blessing

First, believe the blessing of fearing the Lord:

> Blessed is everyone who fears the LORD,
>     who walks in his ways!
> You shall eat the fruit of the labor of your hands;
>     you shall be blessed, and it shall be well with you.
> Your wife will be like a fruitful vine
>     within your house;
> your children will be like olive shoots
>     around your table.
> Behold, thus shall the man be blessed
>     who fears the LORD. (vv. 1–4)

This first part of the psalm, verses 1 to 4, is proclaiming the blessing of fearing God so that you believe it and fear God yourself. "This is how it is!" the psalm is saying, and, "Blessing comes from fearing God! Fruitfulness is the result of fearing God! Will you believe that, accept that, live like that?" It concludes, "Behold, thus shall the man be blessed who fears the LORD" (v. 4) so that we believe that blessing comes from fearing God.

### Defining "Blessing"

In the Bible, being blessed is being truly happy because you are living in a state that God declares to be the best way to live. Blessing is declarative: "Look, that is the *best* way to live!" It is also experiential: "Look, that is the *happy* way to live!" This psalm says that blessing, both the state and the experience of being blessed, comes from fearing God. It does not say, "Blessed is everyone." Nor does it say, "Blessed are people of above-average IQ." The blessing is not for those who are good-looking enough to appear on TV. The blessing is for those who fear God.

*Describing Fearing God*

Verse 1 specifically describes what it means to be someone who "fears the LORD." Those who fear the Lord are also all those "who walk in his ways." So a God-fearing person and a God-fearing family walk in God's ways, which means to follow what God teaches. Jesus makes a similar point when he says that those who genuinely love him will be those who do what he says: "Whoever has my commandments and keeps them, he it is who loves me" (John 14:21). "Fearing God" is not a bumper sticker slogan but requires godly action to be genuine.

Now, that description of fearing God (and loving Jesus) could be an encouragement to you if you grew up in a religious family that was not as good or fun as Psalm 128. Because the Bible defines fearing the Lord as walking in his ways, those who say they fear the Lord must walk in his ways, and those who do not walk in his ways do not fear God. Therefore the blessing of Psalm 128 is only true for those who genuinely fear God, not for all those who only say they fear God but do not truly fear him. These first four verses describe the blessing of a true God-fearing family.

From fearing God, verse 2, comes fruitful working, "labor," and being "blessed" that "it shall be well with you." Fearing God does not sprinkle pixie dust on your life, but given that God is creator, sustainer, and provider of all, to walk in his ways will most of the time (all other things being equal) create a life of happiness and fruitfulness. This is the normal blessing of fearing God. There can be blessing in suffering, and in our fallen world there is always potential for disappointment, but while we must balance this teaching here with books such as Job, we must not mute it entirely. There is real blessing for those who fear God.

Also from fearing God comes the blessing of a wife like a "fruitful vine" (v. 3). She will not be unfulfilled or repressed, barren or bitter, but flourishing. Some medical conditions make childbearing impossible, but this fruitfulness embraces the whole person as well as the womb. "Your children will be like olive shoots" (v. 3). The image of olive shoots is not as familiar as the vine. The point is that when you cut olive shoots, they grow up again very quickly. Today someone might say, "Your children are growing like weeds." An image of weeds may carry less positive overtones than that of olive shoots, but the point of rapid growth and resistance to setbacks is the same. "They're just springing up everywhere." Life. Abundance. Fruitfulness. That is the blessing on offer to those who fear God.

Then the psalm summarizes its point of believing the blessing of fearing God by asserting, "Behold, thus shall the man be blessed who fears the LORD" (v. 4).

### Applying the Blessing of Fearing God in Family Life

I think it was James Dobson who said, "The other man's grass may be greener, but it still needs mowing." Adulterous affairs are a mirage, a cruel lie. Adultery is like a man dying of thirst in the desert who sees an oasis and uses his last strength to crawl to it, only to find that it is a mirage. Affairs always begin with excitement and a thrill; otherwise they would not begin. But soon enough, one day she has a headache, he runs out of money, and you will look back and wish you had decided to stay for the sake of the children. There was research done by Cambridge University that showed that children of divorced parents are damaged more by divorce than by their parents' death. I do not mean to discourage you if you are the child of divorced parents or if divorce is in your past, for a "bruised reed he will not break" (Matt. 12:20). I do want to put a strong barrier in front of those who are facing temptation. Adultery, Proverbs says, is like carrying fire next to your chest, or walking on hot coals (Prov. 6:27–28). You are bound to get burnt. There are more and more opportunities for even a fantasy lifestyle that is a cruel mirage. We need to make a covenant with our eyes, like Job (Job 31:1).

We may perhaps find it helpful to consider Agatha Christie's view of the ideal husband. According to her, an ideal husband for a wife is an archaeologist: "The older she gets, the more interested he is in her." So we do not live in a fantasy world; we live in the world of commitment, believing that at the end of life, as at the beginning, family is the place of fruitfulness, for "children's children" (v. 6).

But it is more than simply individual temptations these days; it is the whole approach of Western society that is being influenced to move away from the traditional model of marriage, saying that it is not a place of fruitfulness but a place of repression. To counteract the pressure of our contemporary culture, it is helpful to look at some of the data.

*Consider Some Data*

Harvard sociologist Carle Zimmerman in his book *Family and Civilization*, originally published in 1947, predicted an inevitable social decay that would result from undermining traditional models of families.[1] He had a series of eleven steps. You can find the book and see that the steps are remarkably prophetic. His list included marriage losing its sense of sacredness in a culture, which leads to the traditional meaning of the marriage ceremony being lost, which then leads to increasing public disrespect for parents, acceleration of juvenile delinquency, growing acceptance of other models of relationship, and increasing crimes and sex perversions. As I write, we seem closer to Zimmerman's prediction than many in 1947 probably ever thought likely.

Edward Gibbon, in his classic work *The Decline and Fall of the Roman Empire*, had a very similar list of cultural decay.[2] The undermining of the dignity and sanctity of the home would lead to increasing taxes and spending of public money for bread and circuses, a mad craze for pleasure, with sports becoming more exciting and more brutal, and the building of gigantic armaments, when the real enemy is the moral decadence of the people, and then the decay of religion, with faith fading into a mere form. Those of you who are historians will know that Edward Gibbon is hardly the poster child for orthodox Christianity, and yet he observed the importance of marriage and family for social health.

More recently, sociologist Mark Regnerus has shown there is demographic pressure to cohabitate and that has damaging results on society. He argues that men are naturally motivated by the desire to provide and protect and procreate. However, since 1971 the income of American young men has declined by 21 percent. And only 43 percent of American undergraduates at university today are men. This means that the connection between productive work and procreation is being

---

[1] Carle C. Zimmerman, *Family and Civilization*, 2nd abridged edition (Wilmington, DE: Intercollegiate Studies Institute, 2008).
[2] Edward Gibbon, *Decline and Fall of the Roman Empire*, 1776–1778.

cut. Demographically some men do not have to be married, so they are not. Other men cannot provide, so they cannot be married. The combination encourages cohabitation, and what happens is young men become unmotivated to protect or provide. And if that doesn't persuade you to commit to the traditional model of marriage, consider this: the *Journal of Marriage and Family* discovered that those who live together before they are married are less likely to stay together.[3]

I am laying all this out because I want to show you that the postmodern idea that we can reinvent our sexuality, that we can reinvent the model of families, and that this will have no negative impact on civilization is miscued. And I want to show you that, instead and by contrast, the blessing of this psalm for the family, for "Zion" (v. 5) or God's people, for "children's children" or the progress of the gospel down the generations, is true and to be believed therefore. The psalm is asking you to believe this blessing of marriage and family for those who fear God.

## Receive the Blessing

Second, receive the blessing:

> The LORD bless you from Zion!
>    May you see the prosperity of Jerusalem
>    all the days of your life!
> May you see your children's children!
>    Peace be upon Israel! (vv. 5-6)

Verses 5 and 6 are asking us to receive the blessing that verses 1 to 4 have described. Verses 5 and 6 begin with a prayer for the reader to be blessed: "The LORD bless you from Zion" (v. 5). As verses 1 to 4 were asking you to *believe* the blessing, so this second part of the psalm, verses 5 and 6, is now asking you to *receive* the blessing described in the first part of the psalm. "If fearing God is that good," it says, "if family is that 'blessed,'" then may God give you that blessing!" We have had the *fides* of verses 1 to 4, and now we have the *sacramentum* of verses 5 and 6. The psalm is asking God to bless your marriage and your family.

---

[3] Alfred DeMaris and K. Vaninadha Rao, "Premarital Cohabitation and Marital Instability in the United States: A Reassessment," *Journal of Marriage and Family* 56 (1992): 178–90.

*Not a List of Ten Steps to a Perfect Family*

The psalm is *not* saying that all marriages and families that follow Christian principles are perfect or painless. I want to share with you part of a Christmas letter that was sent to me from a so-called perfect family:

> Dear friends,
>
> Our year has been a *discouraging* one. Simon, age fifteen, is disappointed because he must defer his entrance to Oxford University for another whole year! Angela, age thirteen, is trying to decide between a tour with the Chicago Symphony Orchestra and going to the Olympics on the US Gymnastics Team. Do pray for wisdom for her as she cuts this Gordian knot! William, age twelve, was awarded the youth group "Mr. Humility Prize," but he refused out of consideration for the feelings of his friends. I don't know, with children like these it does make you wonder, doesn't it? Hope all is well with you.
>
> Yours sincerely,
> A perfect family

Does that sound vaguely familiar? Of course it is a made-up prayer letter, but it can be irksome to be told how excellently the year has gone for other families, though you know you should not be jealous, and probably some people feel your family is doing marvelously. But verses 5 and 6 are not a prayer letter that tells you how wonderful everything already is; they are a heartfelt prayer (whether by letter or not) that asks God to bring blessing. It is not a list of how-to steps, rules, or bullet points that can falsely give the impression that "if you follow these steps everything will be fine." The author of the psalm knows that we live in a broken world, and even the best of families experience brokenness from time to time, a brokenness that easy how-to guides rarely solve satisfyingly.

*A Prayer, Not a Rule Book*

No, this part of the psalm is a prayer, not a rule book. Having described the blessing for those who fear God, in verses 1 to 4, it now asks for that blessing, for marriage is a kind of *sacramentum*, that is, there is a sacredness to it. (I am not advocating for a particular Latin translation of *sacramentum* that means "formal religious sacrament." I am saying that marriage and family are intended to be divine blessings.)

*Marriage Is Meant to Be the Whole Story of the Bible in Miniature*

You see, in one way you have to read verses 5 and 6 in the light of the whole story of the Bible. That story begins in a garden where marriage was "good" or "blessed." Love was rejected there and love was spoiled. Love pursued the rebel, "loved the loveless that they might lovely be," by willing sacrifice in a different garden named Gethsemane. And finally there will be a marriage in heaven. All of that means that your very own, very normal, very human marriage is intended to be a "mystery" referring to *that* sacred marriage (Eph. 5:32). Your family is a potential place of such sacredness. It is a possible "zone of *sacramentum*," a "zone of sacredness" where the Lord's blessing resides, if you fear him by walking in his ways. You might say, family is meant to be a sanctuary.

Once again, I know that no family is perfect and that every family struggles sometimes. Even if you believe the blessing here described and ask for God's blessing on our families in this way, as I encourage you to do, it does not mean that family life will necessarily be what you think of as easy. For instance, John Wesley, famed evangelist of the eighteenth century, became romantically embroiled with a woman. Mrs. Mary Vazeille was a widow with seven children. They fell in love. They got married in haste, and they repented at leisure. She opened his letters. One time she even dragged him across the floor by his hair. Wesley perhaps concluded that at least his unhappy home life encouraged him to not mind traveling away from home for the gospel. That is what the contemporary John Berridge thought.[4] If that has a touch of irony about it, consider the bigger picture. In other words, this means that a bad family experience can still be a part of one of the greatest revivals the world has ever seen. This psalm is not saying, "If you follow

---

[4] Michael Watts, *The Dissenters, From the Reformation to the French Revolution*, vol. 1 (Oxford: Clarendon, 1978), 419–22.

this, you'll be perfect." It is saying, "Follow this so that there will be abundance for you, for your children, and for your children's children."

But if you do *believe* the truth of verses 1 to 4 and *receive* the blessing of verses 5 to 6, it will make a huge difference. It will mean blessing for you, your marriage, your children, your grandchildren, and "Zion" (God's people)—a blessing for family, church, and the progress of the gospel down the generations.

A Song of Ascents.
"Greatly have they afflicted me from my youth"—
    let Israel now say—
"Greatly have they afflicted me from my youth,
    yet they have not prevailed against me.
The plowers plowed upon my back;
    they made long their furrows."
The Lord is righteous;
    he has cut the cords of the wicked.
May all who hate Zion
    be put to shame and turned backward!
Let them be like the grass on the housetops,
    which withers before it grows up,
with which the reaper does not fill his hand
    nor the binder of sheaves his arms,
nor do those who pass by say,
    "The blessing of the Lord be upon you!
    We bless you in the name of the Lord!"
—Psalm 129

# 10

# FINDING FREEDOM FROM THE PAST

As you scan your eye down this psalm, you may be somewhat surprised to know that I once preached this passage on the Sunday before Easter, on Palm Sunday. It reminded me a little of the story of the pastor who was getting up to greet his people on Easter Sunday morning and inadvertently began, "Merry Christmas!" Psalm 129—Palm Sunday? Yes, really.

## An Inevitable Question

Of course, this is one of those parts of the Bible where anyone with any degree of sympathy and sensitivity can begin to see why these days some critics of contemporary Christianity, and of the Bible, say that religion can encourage a rather aggressive tendency to our thoughts and even our actions. There are those who say that religion is the cause of all the wars, or that the Bible is hate speech, and the like.

This psalm may not make everyone's list of "imprecatory" psalms (psalms that call upon God to judge), and it is certainly not the most startling of them. But it clearly has elements of that. There is a wish that God would behave in a certain kind of way toward those who have behaved toward the psalmist and Israel and God's people in a certain kind of way. So when you read this psalm, you have to ask yourself a question: what do you do with these raw emotions, with these statements in the Bible? Do those who criticize Christianity and all religion as being inherently violent actually have a point? Is there some element of truth in it? What do we do with these strong, bold statements that are so startling to us and seem strange? How do we deal with these kinds of emotions?

## Avoiding the Question

People have adopted different approaches to tackle those questions. One of the most common is to try to avoid it. You know: only read the bits of the Bible that are noncontroversial—John 3:16 over and over again, and then 1 Corinthians 13, and our favorite bits of the Bible. Let's make sure that any visitor to church hears us talk only about the nice stuff. Of course, that approach does not really work, because most people know there are parts of the Bible that are not so easy to understand. Even with something as central as the cross, someone dies—violently.

These days there are many who criticize atonement theology and say that it merely legitimizes violence by the fact that the atonement was a violent deed. They even look at the victory march of Jesus into Jerusalem and say, "Well, that is actually just a species of either/or exclusivism. You're either for him or you're against him." The kind of judgment statements that Jesus brings, the laments that he speaks over Jerusalem, seem startling to them, if not an outright example of what they mean by saying that religion promotes aggression.

So we cannot just ignore these questions, for people genuinely ask them. We cannot put our head in the sand, blank over parts of the Bible, and say that it is all about love, because there are parts of the Bible that are not all about love. Anyone who reads the Bible will know that sometimes God is described as having wrath against his enemies. So how do you deal with that? How do you answer when there is a *song* here (this is a song, a song of ascent), a song that wishes that people will *not* get blessed? "Oh, may they not be blessed!" sung to the tune of *Greensleeves*. It seems strange or silly, petty, and pathetic. We cannot blithely ignore it.

## Simplistic Rationalization

But if we cannot ignore the question and be a bit like Jefferson, who took a pair of scissors to his Bible and cut out the bits he did not like, the other common approach does not work either. That is, we cannot simplistically rationalize it.

The most obvious example of a simplistic rationalization is to say,

"This is the God of the Old Testament, whereas the God of the New Testament is very different." That is a common idea. Is it right? Well, there are all sorts of difficulties in that attempt to deal with this problem. To begin with, most obviously, are we then saying that God is different between one Testament and the other? Does God change between the Old and the New Testaments? Is he a different kind of God? Really? What about Jesus being the same yesterday, today, and forever (Heb. 13:8)? What about God being eternal, the "unmoved mover," if you like that phrase?

But even more than such simplistic rationalization not making sense at a logical level—that is, it does not fit logically with what we know about God—neither does it make sense when we truly read the Bible. For instance when Paul, in the New Testament, urges the Roman Christians to forgive, to return blessing for cursing, not cursing for blessing, what does he do? He quotes from the *Old Testament*. So Paul writes, "If your enemy is hungry, feed him; if he is thirsty, give him something to drink" (Rom. 12:20), which is a quotation from the Old Testament book of Proverbs (25:21).

In fact, once we begin to read the Bible carefully we find that the Old Testament is full of the revelation of the love of God. The Old Testament tells you that "the LORD is slow to anger and abounding in steadfast love" (Num. 14:18). Indeed one of the key words of the whole Old Testament is *hesed*, meaning the covenant faithfulness and love of God. And at the same time, in the New Testament you find that no one talks of hell more frequently than Jesus (e.g., Matt. 5:22, 29–30; 13:41–43; 25:31–46; Mark 9:42–50; Luke 16:19–31). Or that right at the end of the New Testament, in the book of Revelation, God's wrath against evil is described in frankly scary terms (e.g., 14:17–20).

## Higher than Our Standards, Not Lower

So what we begin to realize is that the solution is not to pick and choose which parts of the Bible we like so they fit into our view of what we want God to be like and therefore make a different kind of idol. When someone is doing Bible study in a small group and he begins by saying, "I like to think of God as . . ."—what *you* like to think of God as? How does *God* like to think of God? It is all rather similar to someone saying that they like to think of you as five foot three when really you are actually six foot one. What gives them the right to decide how tall you are? But worse: at least your overly definitive friend is another human like you. But what gives humans the right to define God?

Instead, then, of picking and choosing the bits that we prefer defined by our own ideas and preferences, consider whether the passage in front of us is saying something bigger and better than we could have conceived, even if it is rather surprising to begin with. Could it be the case that it is saying something not beneath our own moral taste but far above it?

## The Past

First, the past:

> "Greatly have they afflicted me from my youth"—
>    let Israel now say—
> "Greatly have they afflicted me from my youth,
>    yet they have not prevailed against me.
> The plowers plowed upon my back;
>    they made long their furrows." (vv. 1–3)

Verses 1 to 3 describe the person who has been afflicted. This psalm speaks in the voice of an individual ("Greatly have they afflicted *me*," v. 1), and yet all the people ("let *Israel* now say," v. 1) are encouraged to speak the psalm. Does that mean that this affliction is common to all people, is experienced by one person whom all are to identify with, is Israel's suffering dramatized through an individual testimony, is a messianic prophecy of Christ (identified as Israel), or all of the above? I suppose opinions will vary, but the "all of the above" option would be typical of the historical rigor and christocentric nature of the Bible. At the very least this person is not someone who is acting solely in a private, selfish role. The psalm is talking about God's people Israel and about someone who is identified closely with them and honored by them. What happened to this individual (and we shall see it was terrible) closely concerns the honor of God himself. That is almost a rule with such imprecations, to the degree that this psalm is imprecatory.

When the Bible says, "God will judge," it is God's Word saying that he will judge, not some jumped-up wannabe trying to get vengeance.

This person has experienced difficult suffering in his past. He has been "afflicted" all the way back to "my youth" (v. 1). The affliction is not circumstantial but a personal attack; it is "they" (v. 1) who have afflicted him. They have afflicted him "greatly" (vv. 1–2). This affliction is then underlined to emphasize how bad it was: "Greatly have they afflicted me from my youth" (v. 1), and then again, "Greatly have they afflicted me from my youth" (v. 2). Though this affliction is so severe it bears repeating, this person has not been defeated. There is hope despite the difficulty, for while the suffering is personal ("they" afflicted, not the situation), is real (an "affliction," not an inconvenience), is serious ("great," not minor), and is long lasting ("from my youth," not only yesterday), he can still say, "Yet they have not prevailed against me." This afflicted person is a survivor, if not a savior.

In case anyone is still not convinced that his triumph of adversity is remarkable, verse 3 specifies just how bad his affliction was: "The plowers plowed upon my back; they made long their furrows." It is perhaps picture language. "All this lifelong affliction," he could be saying, "feels like I have been run over by a plow." It is possible, though, that these words are referring literally to the practice of some in the ancient world to mistreat captives by using farming implements. Prisoners of war were literally "plowed upon their backs" with plows. The person who was afflicted may be saying that they flouted the rules of the Geneva Convention. He was tortured.

*Crimes against Humanity*

Once you consider that possibility, you begin to realize that this is not simply addressing some relatively minor issue that happened in the psalmist's childhood. This is about the truly horrible afflictions of life, even the war zones of our day. How do you help a society move beyond those things? How can captor live with captive when the captivity ceases?

People have tried different things. They have tried the Nuremberg trials. Is that the solution? Or is the solution the Truth and Reconciliation Commission that happened after apartheid in South Africa? Or is the solution a sort of general amnesty? Do we sweep the matter under the carpet? Or do we let it all come out and find healing through some mutual gestalt therapy of truth telling? And if that is the case, how do we know whether it is really the truth? Or do we seek justice through proper procedure in the legal system, the human law courts? And if that is the way to do it, how does that procedure not become the victor's justice now so that the previous victims become the new victimizers, and the vicious cycle keeps on turning? Or is the solution higher and better than we could conceive?

## Freedom from the Past

Second is freedom from the past:

> The LORD is righteous;
>     he has cut the cords of the wicked. (v. 4)

The solution is found in two words in the original Hebrew and four in the English translation: "The LORD is righteous" (v. 4). So the psalmist had had this great affliction (v. 1) from his youth. It is such extreme suffering that it is repeated, and "greatly" is put in the emphatic position to make it clear how bad it was. "Greatly . . . greatly," repeated, from his youth. It is not so bad that he did not survive. Otherwise, the psalmist would not have written the psalm. "Yet they have not prevailed against me" (v. 2). He is fighting on. He is still breathing. But, nonetheless, the affliction overshadows his present. It is going round and round in his mind; he repeats it over and over again. "Greatly have they afflicted me from my youth," he says. Then once more, "Greatly have they afflicted me from my youth."

Why does it keep on going round in his mind? Well, he feels like he has been stabbed in the back, plowers plowing his back with long furrows, and such betrayal is hard to forget. Then in verse 4 comes the solution: "The LORD is righteous; he has cut the cords of the wicked." This is the same plow theme. The idea, I think, is that the cords attaching the farm implement to the plow that the oxen were pulling have been cut, so the psalmist is free.

*Forgiveness Is Not Easy*

Now when you really begin to delve into this statement, "The LORD is righteous; he has cut the cords of the wicked," you begin to see that the easy answer is too easy. It is easy to say that the solution is that you have to forgive those people who afflicted you. Forgiveness is, of course, the right answer, but when you just say it like that, there is an assumption that forgiveness is fairly easy, and forgiveness is anything but easy. Obviously, Christians are called to forgive. Obviously, our model is Jesus, who from the cross said, "Father, forgive them" (Luke 23:34), and was followed by the first Christian martyr, Stephen, who prayed very similarly when he was killed (Acts 7:60). But how? How do we actually live in the present and not be stuck in the past? How do we become released from being victimized so as not to live as a victim? How do we forgive? It is not easy.

An interesting example of the profundity of this passage for this issue of moving on comes from a book by Simon Wiesenthal. He was a Jewish man who wrote a book called *The Sunflower: On the Possibilities and Limits of Forgiveness*. He recalls in this book how, as a Jew, he was asked by a former Nazi who had committed atrocities to come to that former Nazi's deathbed. There he was at the deathbed, as a representative of the Jewish people, and the former Nazi asked Wiesenthal, having told him all that he had done, to forgive him. Wiesenthal paused, and then he walked away. He could not do it. The book that Wiesenthal authored is a collection of essays answering the question, "What would you do?" Well, what would you do? Perhaps walking away sounds easy to you, but then have you really walked away if you have not forgiven? Has a new day really begun?

There is a story of three US former servicemen who were standing in front of the Vietnam Veterans Memorial in Washington, DC, the capital of America, and one asked his friend, "Have you forgiven those who held you prisoner?" And, of course, it is a big question, and in the end the other replied, "You know, I will never forgive them." And then his friend said to him, "Well, it seems that they still have you in prison then, don't they?"

*The Lord Will Judge*

You see, it is easy to talk about forgiveness. It is not so easy to do it. How do you actually escape from the prison of your past? Because "the LORD is righteous; *he* has cut the cords of the wicked" (v. 4). Let God be the judge, so "judge not, that you be not judged" (Matt. 7:1). Let God take revenge: "Vengeance is mine, I will repay, says the Lord" (Rom. 12:19). You can leave it up to God because "the LORD is righteous." Not forgiving is far from neutral, at least if that refusal to forgive is intransigent. Forgiveness requires accepting that *only* God is righteous, and you and I are not. Forgiveness necessitates the faith to believe that we are righteous only with God's righteousness, so that we do not store up the wrongs done to us like bargaining chips. Forgiveness comes from saying, "God is the judge," and, "The LORD is righteous."

## Model and Warning

Third is model and warning:

> May all who hate Zion
> be put to shame and turned backward!
> Let them be like the grass on the housetops,
> which withers before it grows up,
> with which the reaper does not fill his hand
> nor the binder of sheaves his arms,
> nor do those who pass by say,
> "The blessing of the LORD be upon you!
> We bless you in the name of the LORD!" (vv. 5–8)

These final verses of the psalm are both a model to copy and a warning to heed. As the psalmist finds resolution through the truth that "the LORD is righteous," he now moves beyond his past in a way that at the same time is to be both emulated and avoided.

*A Model of Honesty with God*

One aspect of the model is, I think, his frankness—the emotional honesty, the reality, the authenticity. It is strong language. He is borrowing from the agricultural images of his day to describe how he wants those who "hate Zion" to "be put to shame" (v. 5). He is saying that he feels like he wants those who have oppressed him to have no fruitfulness.

Their harvest, he hopes, will be stunted. It will not be like a prairie field of wheat bending gloriously in the sun. No, he hopes it will be like grass growing momentarily on the mud roofs of the East ("grass on the housetops," v. 6), which when summer comes quickly burns up. And so there will be no harvest to gather; the "reaper does not fill his hand nor the binder of sheaves his arms" (v. 7). Therefore the traditional greeting that was given to harvesters, "The LORD be with you!" with the familiar reply, "The LORD bless you" (Ruth 2:4), would not take place. As the lack of harvest becomes apparent, he hopes that "those who pass by" (v. 8) will not give that greeting because there is no crop. Instead he wants there simply to be a shocking silence, like Scrooge wanting no one to say, "Merry Christmas."

As prickly as the language is, no one could fault him for not being honest with God. In some ways, then, he remains a model of such honesty. He not only leaves judgment to God ("the LORD is righteous," v. 4); he also continues to practice emotional frankness with God. He is not one to bottle it up or stew over it inside, pretending he does not feel like this. Nor, though, it should be said, is he having a damaging public meltdown, shouting in anger while at the office or at home. This is between him and God, in devotional honesty, recorded partly as a model.

Here then is a less common reason why personal times of Bible reading and prayer are important. You can tell God what is honestly going on inside and then encounter God and be brought back to the right place. The sting of this psalmist's feelings are being drawn by God in the devotional realm. He is telling God how he feels, trusting God to discern the right from the wrong in those feelings, leaving it to God ("the LORD is righteous"), so that, as it were, on the other side of those feelings of vengeance, now given to God, comes the possibility of forgiveness. So this is partly a model.

### A Warning about Not Taking Revenge

Yet as soon as you say that this is a model, you begin at once to realize that there is also a warning in these words. It all seems awfully close to petty vindictiveness. This is one reason why we have to have a subtle approach to the different genres of literature in the Bible. Not everything that is felt or said or sung in the Psalms is a model for us to feel or say or sing. So these words here function to some extent like a sign on the road, saying, "Bridge Out. Don't Go Here." This belongs in the Bible, but it is a biblical warning to some degree as well. Some of the Bible, some of the history portions as well as this part of the Bible, is written as warning.

There is a warning here to those of us who have significant power over others. Perhaps you are a business owner or a CEO or a school teacher or a politician. The kind of anger that we find simmering here is what happens when someone feels that he is being kept down or mistreated. When humans are treated as slaves, they are tempted to turn the affliction upon those who have afflicted them. It is only natural. It is the way of things. It is a warning to those who have power (and reason to be grateful if you do not have much power).

It is also a warning to us if we feel we have been afflicted. It is very easy to give in to those feelings and lash out and wish in our hearts that one day our tormentors will get what they deserve. It seems to me that C. S. Lewis is particularly profound here in his reflections on the Psalms when he notices that the kind of vindictiveness we sometimes see in the Psalms is only really possible for someone who has developed a sense of right and wrong. Those who still live in a world where they expect everyone to behave selfishly and think there is no judgment to come can just live as if there is no comeuppance of any kind whatsoever. This, he argues, is a lower and lesser sin, to think there is no truth and no right and no wrong. But for those who realize and have been awakened to the fact that "the LORD is righteous," there comes a greater possibility as well as a greater danger. So Lewis writes, "It is great men, potential saints, not little men who become merciless fanatics. And those who are readiest to die for a cause may easily become those who are readiest to kill for it."[1]

### A Model-Warning Blended

Not that there is any wish for killing here, but then comes the final model-warning blended together. The psalm says, "Nor do those who

---

[1] C. S. Lewis, *Reflections on the Psalms* (New York: Harcourt, 1958), 28.

pass by say, 'The blessing of the LORD be upon you! We bless you in the name of the LORD!'" (v. 8). Those who have been to thousands of Palm Sunday services over the years may recognize some of the strange resonance of these words. I am not saying that those who thronged their way and sang sweet hosannas and said, "Blessed is the king who comes in the name of the Lord," were directly quoting from this passage against the grain, as it were, though the Psalms of Ascent were in all likelihood sung by the pilgrims going up to the feast at Jerusalem. But it is at times like these that you realize, to again quote Lewis, "what a tissue of quotations from [the Old Testament] the New Testament is."[2] With the blessing of Ruth to the harvesters; to the blessing of the king; to the hosanna and blessing of Psalm 118 ("Save us, we pray. . . . Blessed is he who comes in the name of the LORD! We bless you from the house of the LORD," vv. 25–26); to the shouts of acclamation of the crowd on Palm Sunday before their different kinds of cries on Good Friday: this Psalm, with its denial of "the blessing of the LORD be upon you! We bless you in the name of the LORD," is model and warning blended, as you consider Christ's riding in on a donkey.

Is there some Pharisaic spirit here? A self-righteous spirit, the spirit that looks at all the children singing hosanna and tries to make Jesus stop them, but Jesus says if they stop, the stones themselves will cry out. Model and warning. It is a model, because it enables us to trust that God is righteous, to be honest with our feelings before God, and therefore it helps us to draw the sting of our own vengeance. It is also a warning. It is too easy to look at the one who was afflicted for us and instead of blessing him, actually prevent others from blessing him as the Lord, the Righteous One. We have a case of mistaken identity. Instead of personally and privately saying to God, "This is actually how *that* in my past made me feel," we turn on him and stop others from worshiping him. Anger blinds us to see him for who he truly is, our Lord and Savior.

[2] Ibid., 26.

## Redemption

Model. Warning. Redemption. Somehow in this incongruity, congruity is formed. Our past afflictions can be taken to him as the Lord, the judge, who will judge justly, both our afflictions and our affliction of others, both our oppression and the times we have oppressed, both our blessings and our cursing, our acclamation and our cry of "Crucify"— he can take all that and in a moment of atonement transform it.

Getting over your past is really all about having the cross at the heart. Those wounds we have received can be either taken to the cross, and there judged by God as wrong, or left to fester inside as a seed of hell to germinate in eternity. We cannot just let it go, but we can see it crucified, nailed, hung, dead. And so rise to new life and a new future.

A Song of Ascents.
Out of the depths I cry to you, O Lord!
     O Lord, hear my voice!
Let your ears be attentive
     to the voice of my pleas for mercy!
If you, O Lord, should mark iniquities,
     O Lord, who could stand?
But with you there is forgiveness,
     that you may be feared.
I wait for the Lord, my soul waits,
     and in his word I hope;
my soul waits for the Lord
     more than watchmen for the morning,
     more than watchmen for the morning.
O Israel, hope in the Lord!
     For with the Lord there is steadfast love,
     and with him is plentiful redemption.
And he will redeem Israel
     from all his iniquities.
—Psalm 130

# 11

# LIVING GUILT-FREE

A few years ago, Rochelle and I realized we had not been out for an evening together for a *long* time (young children, you see). So with babysitting arranged, off we went to see what was on at the movies. I just picked one that I thought sounded like a chick flick, and I decided this on the basis of the leading actors. There were two actors in the movie who appear sometimes in romances, one in romantic comedies. That was all I knew. So there we were, sitting comfortably in the cinema, my arm around my wife, ready for a nice romantic evening. By the way, the film is called *What Lies Beneath*. And, well, we had *no* idea "what lies beneath." The first half hour of that film is fine. It is quite nice. Then it begins to turn. Then it really gets scary. I think the only reason we did not walk out to try to find a romantic comedy was that we were so shocked. We were rooted to the spot like a deer in headlights. Of course, when we went home we looked on the Internet, read the reviews, and thought, "Well, it *was* a scary movie."

## What Lies Beneath

In a way, what lies beneath is an important consideration when you come to a topic such as guilt. To teach about how to live guilt-free, with appropriate pastoral responsibility, to teach a psalm like Psalm 130, which is one of the great penitential psalms (some believe there are seven of these penitential psalms), is fraught with potential difficulties. That's because some people always seem to feel guilty, whatever you say. They feel guilty because they ate too much ice cream last night. They feel guilty because their parents had unreasonable expectations, and they can never live up to them. On the other hand, while some people seem nearly always to feel guilty, whatever you say, others apparently rarely have any overwhelming sense of guilt at all—I do not mean the sort of people who may be almost clinical, psychopathic, in their lack of guilt feelings but those who seem hardly ever to have any very burdensome feelings of guilt. Such people appear to sail through life thinking they are usually morally right, even if they are not.

So to truly live guilt-free, you have to move beyond a superficial discussion of guilt feelings to address what truly lies beneath in the sense of real guilt. There are, of course, strong feelings in this psalm, but the psalm itself is not really about feelings as such. This psalm is about what a criminologist might term "forensic" guilt, by which he means actual guilt, whether you happen to feel it or not. Subjective or psychological feelings of guilt can sometimes be merely expressions of a certain personality type. But this psalm is not simply describing someone feeling guilty. It is *declaring* someone's guilt and therefore expressing appropriate feelings that come from that guilt. To begin to live guilt-free, you need to identify true guilt.

The psalm, then, first describes this guilt; second, it points to God's forgiveness; and then, third, it shows the hope that comes as a result of living guilt-free.

## Guilt Described

First, guilt is described:

> Out of the depths I cry to you, O LORD!
>   O Lord, hear my voice!
> Let your ears be attentive
>   to the voice of my pleas for mercy! (vv. 1–2)

These "depths" describe the real guilt that lies beneath. The first two verses are not describing social or communal guilt, the kind of guilt that comes when you find that important people you wish to impress disapprove of something you have said or done. No, the conviction is *personal*: "Out of the depths *I* cry to you . . . hear *my* voice . . . *my* pleas for mercy." These first two verses are not describing a petty faux pas or a minor moral misdemeanor. No, the conviction is *deep*: "Out of the *depths* I cry to you," and passionate: "I *cry* to you . . . my *pleas* for mercy."

These first two verses are primarily describing the kind of guilt that is not just personal and profound but also personally and profoundly *offensive to God* himself. So the psalmist is convinced that he must "cry to *you*, O LORD," that you, "O *Lord*," must hear his voice, that "*your* ears" must be "attentive to . . . [his] pleas for mercy." These verses, then, describe guilt that is personal (not the feeling of guilt that comes when society makes you feel guilty), deep (not only feelings, though inevitably expressed with feeling), and specifically against God (not sinning against yourself or another human being).

*Theological Guilt*
All the penitential psalms similarly tell you that human guilt is guilt before God. Most famously, in Psalm 51, where David has committed adultery and murder and has sinned against a lot of people, he still says to God, "Against you, you only, have I sinned" (v. 4). According to the Bible, then, while we can certainly harm other people, and sin against them and ourselves in that sense, ultimately and exclusively ("you, you only") our guilt is before God.

By describing this "theological guilt," the psalm is looking in microcosm at the whole magisterial gospel story. That gospel story goes from original created goodness in Genesis 1 and 2, to the fall in Genesis 3, to final redemption at the cross. So, because of Genesis 3, there is a theological guilt that lies beneath even the nicest smiles. Yet also, as the Bible story unfolds, redemption comes, and this psalm-gospel-in-microcosm shows that redemption too.

*True Conviction of Guilt Is Good*
In fact, these two verses, Psalm 130:1–2, specifically indicate that true guilt has the larger gospel story of redemption in mind in a couple of intriguing ways.

First, the psalmist says it is "out of the depths" (v. 1) that he cries. "Depths" is the first word in the psalm for emphasis. The psalm is sometimes called *de profundis*, meaning "from the depths." *De profundis* imagines being submerged under water. The Israelites feared the sea, and water often appears as something terrible in their literature. "Out of the depths," though, may well have as its background a particular depths out of which they were rescued, a specific sea through which they crossed, that is, the Red Sea. They were in the depths, yet God rescued them (see Exodus 14–15, specifically the "deeps" of 15:8). To call, then, from the depths is not a last despairing gasp of a drowning man; it is a confident call of a child of God believing that as God rescued his people from Egypt, so he will rescue him.

Second, the phrase "Let your ears be attentive to the voice of my pleas for mercy" (v. 2) is a quotation from the commissioning prayer of Solomon's temple (2 Chron. 6:40). That prayer asks God to be "attentive" to the call of his people when they come and humble themselves, repent of their sins, and cry out to God. It asks that he would hear their prayer, forgive their sins, and heal their land. So this cry in the psalm, for God to be attentive to the psalmist's call, is not a loud shout without much expectation of being heard, like a person bellowing in a lonely desert. This is the cry of someone grasping onto a specific promise of God (2 Chron. 7:15), like a child saying to his father, "You promised if I was truly sorry you would forgive me."

These two references may seem a little subtle to the modern reader, but we have to remember how familiar those two stories would have been to the original hearers. The story of the crossing of the Red Sea and of the dedication of the temple to which the pilgrims were journeying would have lived in their memories. They were the classics of the original hearers of the psalm, like someone citing the Apostles' Creed, or mentioning the American Constitution, or quoting Shakespeare, or like a sports fan referencing how his favorite team won a national competition fifty years ago with a brief sentence or two: "Remember *that* score?" "Out of the depths" and "Be attentive to my call" are references that breathe redemption from guilt.

So true conviction of guilt does not despair, because you know God will hear your prayer. That is why Paul differentiates firmly between godly grief and worldly grief (2 Cor. 7:10). Godly grief "produces a repentance that leads to salvation without regret," the joy that comes from living guilt-free. Worldly grief "produces death" as it wallows in feeling sorrowful but is not actually repentant. This psalm is saying, "As the Israelites were freed from Egypt when they crossed the Red Sea, as

God promised that he would hear his people, so you too can know that God will hear you if you truly cry to him."

*Different from Common Attitudes toward Guilt*

Perhaps you can see the difference between this description of guilt and some common attitudes toward guilt today. This conviction of guilt is not puritanical, not a manipulative power game, not merely psychological. There is such a thing as real, theological conviction of guilt. That conviction of guilt is, in the Bible's way of thinking, as objective a form of guilt as when someone breaks the law of the land. Actually it is more so: this guilt is not only breaking the law; it is personally offending the One who made all law. This is not like getting a speeding ticket; it is like spitting in the face of the president; not a parking fine, but punching the queen. Yet, this conviction "out of the depths" is certain that God will be "attentive." Conviction of guilt is the necessary preliminary to redemption.

## God's Forgiveness

Second is God's forgiveness:

> If you, O LORD, should mark iniquities,
>     O Lord, who could stand?
> But with you there is forgiveness,
>     that you may be feared. (vv. 3–4)

Verse 3 asks the hypothetical question, if the Lord does not forgive people (or if he "should mark iniquities"), who would be able to stand, that is, who could stand before God claiming to be righteous? The answer to that question, of course, is that no one could stand if God "should mark iniquities." Jesus's exposition of the Ten Commandments makes this crystal clear. People may say they have not committed murder, but they have hated, which for Jesus means the same (Matt. 5:21–22). People may say they have not committed adultery, but they have lusted, which for Jesus means the same (Matt. 5:27–30). For Paul, it was the tenth commandment ("Do not covet") that showed him how far short of the mark he was (Rom. 7:7). As, then, "none is righteous" (Rom. 3:10), Psalm 130:3 rightly assumes that if God does not forgive, no one can stand. But wonder of wonders, God does forgive: "But with you there is forgiveness, that you may be feared" (v. 4).

### The Forgiveness-Fear Connection

That God is feared because he forgives is a strange way to finish the sentence. More naturally, you might expect it to conclude by saying, "With you there is forgiveness, that you may be *adored*." Or, cynically, "With you there is forgiveness, that I can get away with my favorite sin over and over again." But to conclude, ". . . that you may be feared"? It is an unexpected phrase, and a lot of people struggle to understand it. Evidently that struggle is nothing new, for some of the ancient records pondered enough to suggest ". . . that you may be seen" as an alternative, or simply left the difficult phrase out altogether. What does this really mean? Why is it that with God there is forgiveness and therefore he is feared?

It may become clear if you underline the word "you": "with *you* there is forgiveness"; that is, with *God* there is forgiveness; therefore he is feared. You see, this verse gives the lie to one of the cardinal doctrines of our age, namely, that if people are feeling guilty, they need to "forgive themselves." That secular doctrine of forgiveness removes God. It is saying that when you have sinned, you have sinned against self, not God. Psalm 51:4, if written in the style of this teaching of our day, would not say, "Against you, you only, have I sinned," but instead, "Against *me, me only*, have I sinned." When someone says, "I cannot forgive myself," they may mean that they still feel bad. But if they mean what they say, then they mean that their self is their god. If that sounds strong, consider one Friedrich Nietzsche, who thought that if we say that it is our own forgiveness that counts, then we are making ourselves godlike. The conclusion is alarming, but the logic is sound. What we are saying, if we are saying we have to forgive ourselves ("I've just got to forgive myself!"), is, "I am god, and I decide who is forgiven." But, no, "with *you* there is forgiveness."

Martin Luther describes it from the other side. He says that if we think our own merits (that is, the good things that we do) would lead to our forgiveness, then we would live with the "presumption of merits" and not bother giving much attention to God. In other words, if you did not need forgiving, what then would you need God for? The "presumption of merits" would mean that you do not need to be forgiven, and therefore you do not need to fear God, and therefore you do not need to serve him.

Or look at it through Jesus's illustration in Luke 7:36–50. There is Jesus, at dinner, and a woman of ill repute comes in and begins to weep at his feet. She takes her hair and uses it to dry his feet, having wet them with her tears. All of the Pharisees and the religious leaders are shocked because she is a woman of ill repute. Jesus tells a story to explain: a moneylender was owed by two debtors, one for a large sum of money and the other for a much smaller amount. The moneylender canceled the debt of both. "Now which of them will love him more?" Jesus asks (v. 42). The answer, of course, is the one who had more debt canceled. Jesus then explains that this woman, a "sinner" (v. 39), had her sins forgiven, for her great love is a sign of the great debt that was cancelled, whereas those with little to forgive love little.

*How to Motivate People to Serve*

If you want to motivate people to serve God, you preach the forgiveness of God. You tell people that with God there is forgiveness, and therefore he is feared. You tell the alcoholic, the workaholic, the adulterer, the liar, the thief, the angry person, the covetous person, the Pharisee, and the prostitute that with God there is forgiveness. And when they really believe and accept that, the whole game changes. Suddenly God is no longer the hard taskmaster; he is the one you will do anything for. He forgave you. You are his. Always. Every part of you. Every aspect of your life is now his. Why? With him is forgiveness. It is the fundamental foundational need of every human being. Forgiveness is with God (and him alone), and therefore you fear him.

## Hope

Third is hope:

> I wait for the LORD, my soul waits,
>   and in his word I hope;

> my soul waits for the Lord
>> more than watchmen for the morning,
>> more than watchmen for the morning.
> O Israel, hope in the LORD!
>> For with the LORD there is steadfast love,
>> and with him is plentiful redemption.
> And he will redeem Israel
>> from all his iniquities. (vv. 5–8)

The psalm now says, "I wait for the LORD" (v. 5), which might surprise you, because after "with you there is forgiveness" (v. 4), you expect the offer of forgiveness. Instead, the author of the psalm transitions from the statement that God is the one who forgives to a future longing for God's redemption. The strength of his waiting is confirmed by the addition, ". . . my soul waits" (v. 5), "soul" suggesting that the very deepest part of him is waiting.

Immediately he tells you that though this waiting is passionate, it is certainly not forlorn or hopeless: ". . . and in his word I hope" (v. 5). So the psalm testifies to a key principle of spiritual health, namely, deliberately and decisively placing hope in God's Word. Then he says once more, "My soul waits for the Lord" (v. 6), confirming the impression that his waiting is eager. Indeed, to him this waiting feels even "more than watchmen for the morning" (v. 6). It is so eager that it borders on the impatience of a night guard looking at the time as he longs for morning to arrive. He repeats that image of readiness: "more than watchmen for the morning" (v. 6), as if struck by the exact likeness of his waiting being even more than watchmen over-ready for the morning.

Then, having opened the deepest part of his heart for inspection and shown there hope, he now tells all God's people that they should also have hope: "O Israel, hope in the LORD!" (v. 7). This experience of hope cannot remain his alone; like all genuine experiences of God, it flows out beyond individual excitement to corporate congregational witness to all the people. He wants to assure everyone that hoping in God is not pointless: "For with the LORD there is steadfast love, and with him is plentiful redemption" (v. 7). Hope in God because his love is not fickle or wayward but reliable and consistent and guaranteed. Hope in God because his redemption is not merely sufficient or just about adequate, but abundant, bountiful, lavish, and sumptuous. God's "stead-fast love" and "plentiful redemption" mean that Israel can be certain that God will redeem her from all her sins—not just the minor ones, the polite ones, the nice ones, or the acceptable ones, but the private ones, the shameful ones, and the serious ones, "and he will redeem Israel from all his iniquities" (v. 8).

Why does the psalm end with hope and waiting? It is possible, I suppose, that it concludes this way because the author of the psalm had not yet found assurance of his forgiveness. Perhaps he knows that "with God there is forgiveness," but he has not yet managed to apply that forgiveness to his own life. Maybe he is waiting to feel forgiven, to know that he himself has been forgiven by God, not just that "with God there is forgiveness." That is possible, but, to my mind, this last part of the psalm does not in the least little bit read like someone who is desperate from a lack of assurance. It reads like someone who is now finally confident. He knows that God has steadfast love; he even uses the special Old Testament term for God's covenant love, his steadfast love, his *hesed*, the love that God has for his people. He is confident that with God there is "plentiful redemption."

What is more, in this last section of the psalm he is not navel gazing but explaining his hope so that he can now advocate for other people to hope similarly. A person stuck in the vicious cycle of not feeling assured (when he should) is not likely to recommend that experience to other people.

No, I think he is now waiting and hoping because he *has been* forgiven. You see, guilt is all about the past. Guilt is about what someone did or did not do, what they said or did not say. Guilt, by its very nature, looks back at the past with regret. If you know someone who seems stuck in the past, by what she wears or by the stories she tells, one explanation could be that "what lies beneath" is guilt. Of course, sometimes people reminisce for entirely normal reasons, and sometimes people long for the past because they feel their life has since become disappointing. But one explanation certainly can be that they are "in the depths"; they are caught in a trap of the past because there is guilt in the past. Like a criminal who returns unavoidably by some psychological compulsion to the scene of the crime, guilty people keep on going over in their mind things that they feel guilty about. It is the way of things.

But once you know you are forgiven, you hope. You begin to move forward. You begin to look to the future. What is more, because with God there is forgiveness, you now tell other people that "with him is plentiful redemption" (that phrase in verse 7 is grammatically similar to "with you there is forgiveness" in verse 4). The future no longer has a menacing aspect. Storm clouds may gather, lightning may strike, night—deepest, darkest night—may come, but you now know (and you tell everyone else who will listen) that the future is bright. God is coming; his redemption is coming. Israel can be confident of it.

Christians can be confident of it too. We know how this echo of redemption, from Egypt to exile to the cross, will finish with the new heaven and the new earth. Once we are forgiven people, we are hoping people, eager, dripping with excitement, about the new day that is to come.

If you want to know what this hope is like, try staying up all night. Wait through the watches of the night and refuse to allow yourself to sleep, not even one little nod of the head. You are on watch, and a sleeping guard is a danger to any city. So you watch and you wait. What does it feel like as the clock ticks in the background, the roads are quiet outside, and everyone else is getting their beauty sleep? What does it feel like as you try to stay awake, knowing that when morning comes you will be able to hit the sack and go to sleep? How do you long for the morning? How much? With what eagerness and excitement? Take that feeling, and realize that this feeling of hope is far more.

A Song of Ascents. Of David.
O Lord, my heart is not lifted up;
    my eyes are not raised too high;
I do not occupy myself with things
    too great and too marvelous for me.
But I have calmed and quieted my soul,
    like a weaned child with its mother;
    like a weaned child is my soul within me.
O Israel, hope in the Lord
    from this time forth and forevermore.
—Psalm 131

# 12

# THE HUMILITY OF GREATNESS

In 2004 William Hung appeared on the televised singing competition *American Idol*. Hung is famous not for doing well but for trying, even though he was shockingly bad. He chose a Ricky Martin hit for his audition, though you might not have known unless you were listening carefully. It was perhaps the worst performance ever recorded on *American Idol*, and that program has screened some terrible singing. One of the judges, Simon Cowell, interrupted him and said, "Look—you can't sing, you can't dance. What do you want me to say?" William Hung's reply endeared him to millions: "I'm just following my dreams." The other two judges smiled at that point. Hung continued, "You know, I've got no professional training." Simon said, "Really? That's the surprise of the century." Hung was an engineer at California Institute of Technology, and his dream was to be a rock star. Perhaps he had been told, "You can be whatever you want to be," and he had taken it literally.

## Who You Were Meant to Be

If so, he is not alone. One survey asked teenagers how much they thought they would earn by the time they reached the age of thirty. In 1999 the average expectation was that they would be earning $75,000 per year. What is revealing about those results is that the average earning of a thirty-year-old American in 1999 was $27,000. The teenagers surveyed expected to earn far more than was likely. Maybe they had also been told, "You can be whatever you want to be." Having dreams, wanting to do well, and trying hard are all indisputable goods. But there is something cruel in the idea that whatever you want, you can have, which is how some apparently interpret the slogan "You can be whatever you want to be." Believing that is bound to create disappointment, which in turn can breed envy or lethargy or both. That well-known phrase, taught in schools and underlying contemporary pop psychology, needs to be reverse engineered by this psalm. Instead of "You can be whatever you want to be" (much less, "You can have whatever you want"), it is saying, "Be who you were made to be." It is advocating for that most unpopular of Christian virtues, what is usually called "humility."

The psalm does not use the word *humility* (perhaps the word had as poor a reputation then as it does now) but instead describes humility in the language of personal experience. The psalmist cannot quite say, "I am humble; be like me," for fear of sounding proud. Instead, the psalmist lets the reader hear the language of his heart so the reader can make up his own mind.

The psalm begins in verse 1 by defining *humility* (for it has always been misunderstood), not just by asserting it. Then in verse 2 the psalm presents humility (for we humans have always needed to be persuaded to even try to be humble). Lastly, in verse 3, the psalm applies humility (for it is one thing to know what it is, another to want it, but quite another to be able to practice humility in daily living). So, first, what is humility? Second, do you want it? And third, how do you attain it?

## 1) What Is Humility?

> O LORD, my heart is not lifted up;
> > my eyes are not raised too high;
> I do not occupy myself with things
> > too great and too marvelous for me. (v. 1)

Rather than an arrogant boast about how humble he is ("humility and how *I* achieved it"), this verse is a personal record of his spiritual state. He is not claiming that he has achieved perfect humility; he is opening the content of his private journal for all to inspect. Only later, in verse 3, does he offer advice, and there he tells Israel to hope in the Lord rather than to be humble like he is. In verse 1 he is sharing, not claiming; he is talking to God, not lecturing us; much less is he boasting . Humility is defined in four ways through this personal journal record of verse 1.

*Humility Focuses on God*

He starts, then, with God: "O Lord," he says. This is a conversation between the psalmist and God, and we are being given the privilege of overhearing it. This straightaway suggests that humility is defined by a focus upon God. The way to avoid the ridiculous and frustrating cycle of recognizing personal growth in humility, only to realize that such recognition is actually proud, is to stop thinking about yourself and start talking to God. A humble person says, "O Lord," not, "Me, myself, and I"—even if, perhaps especially if, the "I" is followed up with a consideration of your own humility.

*Humility Is a Level Heart*

The definition of humility continues with your attitude, your heart. In the Bible, the heart is not only what you think and feel; it is the thinking-feeling unit of the whole person. The Hebrew idea of the heart is different from the sentimental way the word is used today. The heart is thinking as much as feeling; it is your attitude, and so what you "have a heart for" is what you desire, what you truly want. Concerning the psalmist's heart he says, "My heart is not lifted up." Crucially, as this verse defines humility, he is not saying that his heart has been pushed down. Humility is not *low* self-esteem; nor is it having too much self-esteem. Humility is neither too high nor too low; it is level, being who you were made to be. We find the same idea of being level—neither too high nor too low—in verse 2, where the concept behind the words "calmed" and "quieted" is that of an ancient plow plowing a field level. Humility is not too high; your heart is not lifted up. It is level: who I am made to be.

*Humility Is a Level Look*

Not only the heart but also the eyes are level: "My eyes are not raised too high." What people feel inside sometimes seems to appear through their eyes, as the window of the soul. A humble person's eyes are level; they do not look high and mighty. A proud person, by contrast, looks as if he thinks he is cleverer or better than you.

*Humility Is a Level Goal*

Humility is also his goal: "I do not occupy myself with things too great and too marvelous for me." This is not *occupation* in the sense of a job or career but in the sense of his hopes, dreams, and goals. King David, the author of this psalm, had many great matters to be concerned about, but when someone is truly great, he realizes that there are many things far greater than him. The most intelligent men or women understand that the universe is far bigger than their brain, and the greatest politicians realize how little is in their control. People sometimes say that our goals should be SMART: specific, measurable, achievable, realistic, and time-bound. This is saying that his goals are beyond him. The psalmist aims to be who he was made to be.

Humility starts with God, then leads to a level heart, a level look, and a level goal. It is being all that God has made you to be, not "You can be whatever you want to be"; being how God esteems you, not how you are esteemed by self. Humility is being shaped by God in your heart, eyes, and plans; it is an attitude, a look, a dream. It is not being lifted up, like Icarus flying too close to the sun. Neither is it saying, "Do not fly," much less "Do not dream." It is saying, in your heart, eyes, and goals, be who you were made to be, and then you will find the calm and the quiet on offer in verse 2.

## 2) Do You Want Humility?

> But I have calmed and quieted my soul,
>     like a weaned child with its mother;
>     like a weaned child is my soul within me. (v. 2)

This verse presents humility and shames pride so that you would want the one and loathe the other.

*Presenting Humility: "Calmed" and "Quieted"*

The word that introduces this verse, "but," is not meant to suggest that the topic is different from the previous verse ("I have defined humility, *but* now I am going to talk about something else"). Instead it means that this verse is the consequence of the humility of the first verse ("I have defined humility, but now I am going to describe how good it is to be humble"). That is why the Authorized Version, or King James Version, translated the first word as "Surely," to give this sense that the verse is a certain consequence of the previous verse. The result of the humility defined in verse 1 is the sheer happiness of someone who is calm and quiet, "I have calmed and quieted my soul." Remember, the concept behind the words "calmed" and "quieted" is that of an ancient plow plowing a field level. So, because the heart, the eyes, and the goals are now defined by God and who he has made you to be, then comes this plow that plows the field level, and you are calm; you are quiet. Surely this calm and quiet of soul is what you want?

*Shaming Pride: "Weaned"*

In case his readers were still not sure they wanted to take the considerable effort to grow in humility, David now becomes a little, well, rude. The description of being "like a weaned child" can create an inadequate picture for some people, causing them to gloss over the metaphor with the quick glance of over-familiarity. If humility is "like a weaned child," what does that make someone who is proud? David is saying that before he was calmed and quieted by humility, he was, simply put, a screaming baby. Not a toddler but a young baby, a baby not yet through that uncomfortable stage (for parent as much as child) of being weaned. The next time someone confesses to you that he struggles with that religiously permissible sin of pride, try this tactic: "Stop being such a baby!" (Of course, David writes this about himself, so he cannot really be accused of pointing out other people's faults while being blind to his own).

People usually take a completely different approach to pride. Many seem to think that pride is the occupational hazard of being great. "The proud person has done so many wonderful things and achieved so much; it is hard for him not to be proud," the rationalization goes. Pride, in this way of thinking, becomes almost a badge of having achieved something great. We confuse humility with modesty, or mild incompetency. If only pride could be excused so lightly, we might all be able to think better of ourselves! But in reality, truly great people tend to have more than a tinge of humility. When you live in the company of greatness, you very soon realize how small you are, how little you know, what a small fish you are in a big pond.

David is not saying that a proud person is someone achieving much and therefore naturally tempted by pride (so you must excuse his failing). No, the proud person is like a baby. When you were weaned as a child, that was the first time, in normal human development, that you were forced to realize you could desperately want something yet not have it. What then is the proud person like? The proud person has not been weaned. He is regressing to the developmental ego of a nine-month-old baby. That is why he thinks he deserves *his* dreams to come true, because he is like a baby who thinks he deserves his mother's milk. "Waaah!" the baby inside squawks; "I *want* it!" Funny as the picture is of an adult still nursing, that grown person in baby clothes can wreck homes, marriages, businesses, schools, and churches.

Often the proud are anxious, too. They are not weaned and therefore have yet to be calmed and quieted. They have not learned to trust their heavenly Father for other supplies of spiritual nutrients than the ones they want. They are frightened, perhaps, that when they do not have what they want, the alternative will be worse, not better. If you are constantly worried and stressed, could it be pride? Stress may be triggered by demanding responsibilities, but it is not the inevitable co-habitant of executive leadership. King David had a lot to be stressed about, but humility gave him peace and quiet.

Having defined humility (and so answered the question, what is it?), then presented humility (answering the question, do you want it?), he then applies humility (to answer, how do you attain it?).

### 3) How Do You Attain Humility?

> O Israel, hope in the LORD
>> from this time forth and forevermore. (v. 3)

You attain humility by following the example of verse 3.

*A Change of Perspective*

Suddenly everything changes. Verses 1 and 2 were about the psalmist and God. Now, in verse 3, he turns to look at those around him:

"O Israel, hope in the LORD." In fact, this is such a surprising shift that some scholars have wondered whether verse 3 was part of the original text. But that is to take a poetic clunky gear change as evidence for manuscript frailty, when really what we are reading is a revolution of the perspective of the poet. He is no longer thinking about himself. This sudden change—the wheels spin and the car points in the other direction—is exactly what happens when someone becomes humble. Such a person begins to have the greatness of soul to care for other people.

*The Underlying Biblical Principle*

David was calmed and quieted and weaned (at least when he wrote verse 2), and *therefore* he was great enough to call Israel to hope in God. Looking further back, Moses was undoubtedly the greatest leader Israel ever had *because* he "was very meek, more than all people who were on the face of the earth" (Num. 12:3). Our preeminent example in this as in everything else said, "The Son of Man came not to be served but to serve, and to give his life as a ransom for many" (Mark 10:45), *and so* he was exalted to be the "name that is above every name" (Phil. 2:9).

Paul is rarely thought to be an example of humility (more an example of crusty defiance), but actually he bore the mark of humility—contentment: "I have learned in whatever situation I am to be content" (Phil. 4:11), and *consequently*, "I endure everything for the sake of the elect, that they also may obtain the salvation that is in Christ Jesus with eternal glory" (2 Tim. 2:10). This correlation between humility and greatness to serve other people is why Jesus settled the argument about "who was the greatest" once for all by the aphorism, "If anyone would be first, he must be last of all and servant of all" (Mark 9:34–35).

Considering this principle, I think it is no accident that perhaps the greatest-ever preacher in the English language, George Whitefield, took as his life motto "servant of all." So, despite all the slurs that humility has received from the Uriah Heep character in Dickens ("Ever so 'umble," though he was nothing of the sort), or from Churchill ("He was a modest man with a lot to be modest about," though that modesty is really bashfulness, not humility), it could be that the reason why so many do so little of great consequence is that they are proud. The humble person has the greatness of soul to give his life for other people. If you are inactive in Christian service or passive, even lazy, in public responsibilities, could it be that you have not been "weaned"? Perhaps you have not yet arrived at verse 3, where you are serving other people by saying, "Hope in the LORD"?

*Not Just a Result, but a Method*

This verse 3, "O Israel, hope in the LORD from this time forth and forevermore," is, though, not just a *result* of humility; it is a *method* of growing in humility. As so often in the Bible, godly activity is both a result of heart change and a way to produce further heart change. The surest strategy to begin to love the person who annoys you is to start to love him in practice, and the safest method of growing in humility is to start to do humble things. You should not, of course, pretend to be humble when you do such things ("Look at me—see how humble I am!"), but you should do them nonetheless (without drawing any attention to yourself). Washing dishes without being asked or cleaning the floor without being noticed will not make you humble, but if you do humble deeds, it may be the first step toward, as well as the first sign of, humility. Really, all you are doing is following this psalm's model of serving other people by calling on them to "hope in the LORD." You are making a break from verse 2 (still focused on yourself) to verse 3 (now serving other people).

## Conclusion

The humility of greatness, then, is defined by this psalm (a focus on God, which produces a level heart, a level look, and a level goal), presented by this psalm (calmed, quieted, and weaned), and put into practice by this psalm (serving other people by calling them to hope in God). Humility is not inadequacy or low self-esteem but being focused on God and so becoming who you were made to be. Humility gives you the calm and quiet of soul, even in the middle of king-like executive responsibilities, that so many long for and so few find. Humility is put into practice as you serve other people by calling them to hope in God.

Remember, O Lord, in David's favor,
    all the hardships he endured,
how he swore to the Lord
    and vowed to the Mighty One of Jacob,
"I will not enter my house
    or get into my bed,
I will not give sleep to my eyes
    or slumber to my eyelids,
until I find a place for the Lord,
    a dwelling place for the Mighty One of Jacob."
Behold, we heard of it in Ephrathah;
    we found it in the fields of Jaar.
"Let us go to his dwelling place;
    let us worship at his footstool!"
Arise, O Lord, and go to your resting place,
    you and the ark of your might.
Let your priests be clothed with righteousness,
    and let your saints shout for joy.
For the sake of your servant David,
    do not turn away the face of your anointed one.
The Lord swore to David a sure oath
    from which he will not turn back:
"One of the sons of your body
    I will set on your throne.
If your sons keep my covenant
    and my testimonies that I shall teach them,
their sons also forever
    shall sit on your throne."
For the Lord has chosen Zion;
    he has desired it for his dwelling place:
"This is my resting place forever;
    here I will dwell, for I have desired it.
I will abundantly bless her provisions;
    I will satisfy her poor with bread.
Her priests I will clothe with salvation,
    and her saints will shout for joy.
There I will make a horn to sprout for David;
    I have prepared a lamp for my anointed.
His enemies I will clothe with shame,
    but on him his crown will shine."
—Psalm 132

# 13

# WHEN YOU THINK GOD'S PLANS MIGHT FAIL

Perhaps you once made plans to cook a wonderful meal for some guests, but the food turned out to be a disaster. You may remember the feeling of embarrassment when your dinner plans were ruined. Or, if cooking is not your hobby, perhaps instead you made plans to go out for dinner with some friends, only to discover that everyone's favorite item was no longer on the menu. Again you might remember more than a tinge of frustration that the culinary dreams did not come to pass. Nonetheless, such relatively minor disappointments as dinner plans gone wrong are easy enough to forget with a shrug. "The best-laid plans of mice and men go oft awry," as the poet put it.[1] We all know that in the natural course of events, the best-laid plans can be flawed. We know this is true for dinner plans. We know it is true for major life commitments as well. Someone might make plans as a student to follow a certain career, but later she finds as she looks back on her life that everything went in a different direction. Still, even with much more significant disappointments, most people are reconciled to the fact that no one can perfectly plan the future. After all, mathematical equations that attempt to predict earthquakes can themselves be wrong. I suppose in the end we all learn to accept that human plans can go awry.

But what if you do not think they were *your* plans?

## Pointing to the Plan That Does Not Fail

This psalm helps when you think God's plans might fail. I will admit that, at first glance, these verses can appear to be almost a religious form of irrational exuberance. Reading it might feel to you like listen-

---

[1] Robert Burns, "To a Mouse, on Turning Her Up in Her Nest with a Plough," 1785.

ing to someone speak in an overly excited squawk, jumping up and down and gesticulating wildly, when it would be better to cut the monologue in half and make the case logically. But this psalm has a compelling context that explains why it helps.

You see, when God's people returned from exile, they may well have sung this very song when they first saw the ruined city of Jerusalem. On the ascent from Babylon, from exile back to Jerusalem, all these pilgrim psalms were probably especially precious to them. (Some, if not all, of these psalms were written a long time before; certainly the ascriptions to David and Solomon make that ancient claim clear for those specific psalms). It must have been natural for the pious to sing these pilgrim psalms on the great return from Babylon. In fact, if you read the contemporaneous books of Ezra and Nehemiah, you will find strategic excerpts from the Psalms of Ascent to encourage the people in their attempt to rebuild the ruins. So it seems to me that to appreciate how Psalm 132 helps when you think God's plans might fail, it is best to imagine coming step by step closer to Jerusalem.

Imagine singing, "Let us go to his dwelling place; let us worship at his footstool!" (v. 7), then chanting, "For the LORD has chosen Zion; he has desired it for his dwelling place: 'This is my resting place forever; here I will dwell, for I have desired it'" (vv. 13–14), and even humming along happily to, "I will abundantly bless her provisions" (v. 15). Imagine coming around the corner to where the temple was and as the tune thunders and you sing of God's eternal promise to the throne of David dwelling in Zion, you see destruction and ruin instead.

Those who returned from the exile either lived in serious cognitive dissonance, fooling themselves that the words of the psalm did not apply, or else they understood the psalm better than most. Given the remarkable rebuilding they eventually achieved, I suspect the latter is true, even if they may not have appreciated the psalm's far-flung promise of Christ. I suspect they noticed the key to the psalm, the four-time repeated name of David (vv. 1, 10, 11, 17). I suspect they then recalled the familiar story of God's covenant promises to David. And I suspect that as they therefore thought about David, some of them at least overcame their understandable and profound sense of disappointment to put their confidence in the right location, that is, in the plan that does not fail.

In verses 1 through 9 you will find, then, what David said to God (or "an imperfectly located confidence"); in verses 10–12, what God said to David (or "a perfectly located confidence"); and finally, in verses 13–18, what will happen as a result (or "a joyfully located confidence").

## 1) What David Said to God

> Remember, O LORD, in David's favor,
>     all the hardships he endured,
> how he swore to the LORD
>     and vowed to the Mighty One of Jacob,
> "I will not enter my house
>     or get into my bed,
> I will not give sleep to my eyes
>     or slumber to my eyelids,
> until I find a place for the LORD,
>     a dwelling place for the Mighty One of Jacob."
> Behold, we heard of it in Ephrathah;
>     we found it in the fields of Jaar.
> "Let us go to his dwelling place;
>     let us worship at his footstool!"
> Arise, O LORD, and go to your resting place,
>     you and the ark of your might.
> Let your priests be clothed with righteousness,
>     and let your saints shout for joy. (vv. 1–9)

These first nine verses record the vow that David made to God about building the temple and also how that commitment was gainsaid by God, because it was to be Solomon who built the temple, not David. They show you an imperfectly located confidence (David's heartfelt commitment to God), and encourage you in some ways to have that similar determination to do what it takes to grow the kingdom of God but also to move to the next section of the psalm that outlines the perfectly located confidence, which is greater still.

### David's Determination

The psalmist begins, "Remember, O LORD, in David's favor, all the hardships he endured," immediately indicating that David is the key theme of this psalm. "Hardships" here most likely do not mean the physical hardships of David hiding in a cave or his possible battle wounds. The word, I think, refers to what follows in the next verses, that is, David's "vowed" (v. 2) commitment to push forward what he took to be God's plans, whatever it cost him in personal comfort. Specifically, David is not going to sleep until he sees the job done: "I will not enter my house or get into my bed, I will not give sleep to my eyes or slumber to my eyelids" (vv. 3–4). The commitment not to sleep may be hyperbole, an ancient cultural embellishment understood, in context, to mean that he would "pull some all-nighters" if necessary; or it could be literal. But he is probably at least committing to not going *home* to sleep while this task remains undone. A bit like some incoming senators to Washington, DC, bringing stowaway beds to their office, David is saying he is sleeping "under his desk" until the task is completed. This strong determination and commitment is exemplary in some ways, though it is an imperfectly located confidence at this point, as will become clear.

He commits to stay at the office "until I find a place for the LORD, a dwelling place for the Mighty One of Jacob" (v. 5). Jacob specifically is mentioned among other possible patriarchs, probably because Jacob is the right sort of hero for winning against all odds. You might mention Abraham if you want to remind people of patient faith, but if macho faith is your thing, then Jacob is your man. David is saying he is committed to a Jacob-like wrestling match until the job is done. The "dwelling place" is the temple.

Now, when considering verses 6 to 8, some historical context is necessary to not miss the wood for the trees. This is how I see it, though there may be other ways of putting the pieces together, and to each his own opinion. In 2 Samuel 6 we learn that David had brought the ark back to Jerusalem. In a notorious national tragedy the ark had been captured by the Philistines and when released had stayed for a long time in Kiriath-jearim. So, "we heard of it in Ephrathah; we found it in the fields of Jaar" (v. 6), Ephrathah and Jaar probably being well-known nicknames for Kiriath-jearim. The song is recalling this feted moment of David's finally and gloriously bringing the ark back to Jerusalem, to reverse the national tragedy and replace it with community praise and excited dancing, even from David himself. Such was the exuberance on this occasion that the people began to expect yet greater things, that just down the road there would be a new temple to match the new location for the ark: "Let us go to his dwelling place; let us worship at his footstool!" (v. 7).

So at the start of 2 Samuel 7 we learn that after this celebrated triumph of bringing the ark back to Jerusalem, David commits to go one massive step further. He says to the prophet Nathan, "See now, I dwell in a house of cedar, but the ark of God dwells in a tent" (2 Sam. 7:2), a heartfelt determination to build the temple, which is made clearer by Nathan's reply: "Go, do all that is in your heart, for the LORD is with you" (2 Sam. 7:3). Nathan initially agreed with David's plan to build a temple, but after the word of the Lord came to Nathan that night, Nathan relays to David that God has different plans from David's. *David* will not build God a "house," or temple; *God* will build David a house, or dynasty, and it will be David's son *Solomon* who will build the physical temple.

So then when the pilgrims returning from exile say, "Arise, O LORD" (v. 8), they were singing what Moses said every morning when God's people were wandering in the desert and the ark had no temple (Num. 10:35). As the verse carried on, the overtones of what God had planned rather than what David had vowed were there for all who knew the legacy of the temple, just as well as the fans of Manchester United know the stories of Old Trafford: "Arise, O LORD, and go to your resting place, you and the ark of your might. Let your priests be clothed with righteousness, and let your saints shout for joy" (vv. 8–9). Verse 9 is almost a direct quotation from the famous end of Solomon's prayer at the dedication of the temple as it was finally built according to God's (not David's) plan (2 Chron. 6:41).

### Imperfect, but Still Exemplary

David's desire was not a sinful desire. He was zealous, which was good, even though it was zeal without perfect, although certainly some, knowledge. It may have been imperfect, but it was still exemplary in some ways: "I will not give sleep to my eyes or slumber to my eyelids" (v. 4) is a determination to challenge the sluggish Christian. It reminds me of the well-known story of D. L. Moody, who had made a commitment, a vow if you like, to tell someone about Jesus every day. One night he was almost asleep when he realized he had told no one about Jesus that day. He looked out of the window; it was raining. He saw a man standing under an umbrella. Moody rushed downstairs, shared the umbrella, and said to him something like, "You have a shelter against the rain. Do you have a shelter against the coming wrath of God?" Moody did not allow a good night's sleep to get in the way of fulfilling the Great Commission. Nor should we.

Of course, there is a time for sleep, and I think it was Eric Nash (who discipled John Stott) who would winkingly say that "the secret to the Christian life is sleep." Balance is important. And yet so is zeal. If I had to guess, most Christians in the church suffer more from not considering ever losing sleep over the state of the church than from becoming fanatics in danger of losing their marbles out of too great a devotion. Perhaps this imperfect but exemplary model tells you that it is time to put an end to the natural and easy excuses that you cannot get up early enough to read the Bible before you go to work, or that you do not have time to serve in a ministry at church. As a friend once said to me when I complained about not having any time, "You have all the time there is." He was right: it is a question of how you use your time, and for what. Commitment to Christ surely must mean occasional sleep deprivation. Jesus certainly stayed up all night praying, and he got up early to pray.

## 2) What God Said to David

> For the sake of your servant David,
>     do not turn away the face of your anointed one.
> The Lord swore to David a sure oath
>     from which he will not turn back:
> "One of the sons of your body
>     I will set on your throne.
> If your sons keep my covenant
>     and my testimonies that I shall teach them,
> their sons also forever
>     shall sit on your throne." (vv. 10–12)

This confidence is "perfectly located," not because the confidence is perfect but because the location is, namely, what God has planned, not what the people had planned.

It says here, "For the sake of your servant David," so we see that once more David is the key to the meaning of this psalm. "Do not turn away the face of your anointed one"—the "anointed one" is Messiah, Christ, the king. Then, "The LORD swore to David a sure oath from which he will not turn back." There is a carefully crafted cadence between the prayer "do not turn away the face" (v. 10) and the promise "he will not turn back" (v. 11), which underlines that God's plan will not fail.

What did God say to David? David had wanted to build a temple, which we see in the second part of 2 Samuel 7, summarized here in this psalm: "One of the sons of your body I will set on your throne" (v. 11). This is God saying something like, "David, you want to build me a house, but, David, I want to build you a household, a lineage *if your sons keep my covenant*" (v. 12). There is a need for those who followed in David's line to keep God's covenant, to be in it and committed to it, and yet God's ultimate will and his ultimate purpose will prevail, despite what we read about some of their sins and the consequences of those sins in their personal lives. "If your sons keep my covenant and my testimonies that I shall teach them, their sons also"—here's what God says to David—"*forever* shall sit on your throne" (v. 12). So imagine once more that you have come to the temple, and you discover that it is ruined. As you observe the destruction naturally enough, especially if you are singing this very psalm, you are likely to be asking yourself something like, "But how, then, will what God said to David be fulfilled?" And then you hear again the emphasis: ". . . *forever* shall sit on your throne."

This is teaching us that we are to make sure that our confidence is located in God's Word. It is not telling us not to have confidence; it is telling us to make sure that our zeal is based upon knowledge. It is a good thing to commit to serve God wholeheartedly. Get up early. Stay up late. Work hard for God. But make sure your zeal is appropriately located in God's Word. David was not wrong to want to build a temple for God, but he needed to have a bigger picture of where that zeal of his would be fulfilled. His devotion to building a temple would find fruition not just in Solomon's using David's resources, which he had stockpiled to build a massive, impressive temple. But his zeal to build that temple would lead to the anointed one, a son of David's, who would sit on his throne forever and ever.

In fact, so important is our part to play in God's plan that shockingly, for some theologians, the Bible says, "*If* your sons keep my covenant and my testimonies that I shall teach them, [*then*] their sons . . . shall sit on your throne" (v. 12). While God's eternal plan cannot be thwarted by our moral failures, it is inappropriately located confidence to think we can do whatever we like and still receive the blessing of the covenant. God's plan was fulfilled despite the moral failures of some of David's physical descendants, yet those who did not keep his statutes did not sit on his throne. It is all by grace through faith alone, yet that faith, if true faith, will lead to obedience. And if we live in a way that does not keep the statutes, then it shows we have not received grace. If we are not living obediently, what we need to do is make sure our confidence is appropriately located. We need to put our trust in the Son of David, the anointed one, who reigns forever and ever. Not in the temple. Not in David. But in the eternal throne.

To put your trust in this covenant promise is a bit like getting on a train. You board a train to go to a certain city. If you are not following the covenant's teaching, you are not really getting on the train at all. It is inappropriately located confidence to think that you will get to that city by train if you do not get on the train. But when you board the train, there is still more to come. As each station stop goes by, you are waiting for the final destination—the covenant to Abraham, the covenant to David, the covenant to David's son. This psalmist was trusting that God's covenant promise would in the future come about as he traveled on that covenant train.

We know how it did come about. Jesus is frequently called "the Son of David." There are an estimated fifty-eight New Testament references to David. Jesus is the Messiah, that is, the anointed one. He is the king in David's line. Christians do not pray, "Remember David," without thinking that David, and the covenant given to him, takes them to David's greater Son. We do not pray, "for the sake of your servant David," without thinking that it is fulfilled in the servant who came to give his life as a ransom for many. We have an advantage over this psalmist in that we know how this story is fulfilled, how this journey ends: the final destination of the covenant in Jesus.

Yet we too have to look ahead. As we consider the last section of this psalm, from verses 13 to 18, it is obvious that even as we interpret the language here through its covenant fulfillment in Jesus, not every aspect of this description do we now experience. When we are tempted to think that God's plans might have failed, we can check whether our confidence is appropriately or inappropriately located. What does God promise in his Word? Am I putting my trust in Jesus's reign in the church, the progress of the gospel of Jesus Christ, or am I putting my trust in a happy life and a comfortable house? Am I following God with utmost zeal, even to the extent of feeling like I have a little bit of sleep deprivation going on? And is that zeal the sort that is with knowledge? We can do that—make sure our confidence is appropriately located in God's Word, not in our ideas—but as we look at this last part of the psalm, verses 13 to 18, we realize that when we think about David, we need to think not only about what David said to God (inappropriately located confidence), and about what God said to David (appropriately located confidence), but also about what will happen as a result.

### 3) What Will Happen as a Result

For the Lord has chosen Zion;
   he has desired it for his dwelling place:
"This is my resting place forever;
   here I will dwell, for I have desired it.
I will abundantly bless her provisions;
   I will satisfy her poor with bread.
Her priests I will clothe with salvation,
   and her saints will shout for joy.
There I will make a horn to sprout for David;
   I have prepared a lamp for my anointed.
His enemies I will clothe with shame,
   but on him his crown will shine." (vv. 13–18)

These verses are a picture of a reality that is not yet ours. There is abundance of provision. There are no poor. There is endless joy and excitement. There are no more enemies. I will grant you that these verses never say the words *heaven*, or *Jesus's second coming*, or *the new creation*. They do not say it, but they do far more than describe it—they *long* for it. This is like a man in a desert who is thirsty, not someone sitting on his deck with a cool iced drink at his elbow. But the power of this thirst stirs up a similar longing in all of us. We long for abundant provisions. We long for there to be no more poor. We long for shouts of joy.

We long for heaven. It's been my experience that everyone does in some way or another. We, of course, who have the New Testament, who have reached the final destination in the city with Jesus, have far more to say about heaven than did the Old Testament authors. We can talk of the new heaven and the new earth; we can talk of the second coming of Jesus, and the home of righteousness. But even *our* most powerful descriptions are still more evocative than definitive.

This psalm is about David and thinking about David, and it is saying that when you wonder whether God's plans have failed, think of David. Think particularly of his good desire to build a temple, which was fulfilled in ways he had not imagined; and through that desire inappropriately located was revealed to him a promise of a far greater fulfillment than anyone could have dreamed: great David's greater son, the eternal throne of the anointed one.

The end of the psalm takes us beyond all that, not just to the train arriving downtown in the city but to when we get out and explore the city of God. The dwelling of God. Even our best descriptions of that are indeed as evocative as they are definitive. Where will God dwell? Where is this dwelling? It was symbolically in the temple. It is genuinely in the church, the body of Christ. It is fully in the new heaven and the new earth, where, as Revelation puts it, picking up on this language of "dwellings":

> Behold, the dwelling place of God is with man. He will dwell with them, and they will be his people, and God himself will be with them as their God. He will wipe away every tear from their eyes, and death

shall be no more, neither shall there be mourning, nor crying, nor pain anymore, for the former things have passed away. (Rev. 21:3–4)

That evokes longing, does it not? A place with no enemies, no poor, and abundance of provision—the very presence of God himself. And how will this all come about, this abundance for which we all so long and which guarantees us that God's plans never fail? At the end of the book of Revelation:

I, Jesus, have sent my angel to testify to you about these things for the churches. I am the root and the descendant of David, the bright morning star. (Rev. 22:16)

In other words, when you think God's plans might fail, think about David. Think about what he said to God. Let that devotion be yours, but make sure the zeal is with knowledge, that it is appropriately located in God's Word and what he has really and truly promised for you. Be a student of God's Word, therefore, so you can know what God has promised. But go further than that. Follow the trajectory of David and look to the far shore, the distant horizon, the city of God, the dwelling place of God with his people.

Perhaps you might be thinking, *Are you saying that when I fear God's plans might fail, the answer is to just remember that everything comes right in heaven?* No, I am saying, remember David because that will take you to Jesus, that will take you to the church; there you will find a community of joy now and deep longing hereafter. In other words, you will be on the train. And your confidence will be located in what God has promised for you—not irrational exuberance but biblical exuberance based upon the sure and certain covenant plan of God.

A Song of Ascents. Of David.
Behold, how good and pleasant it is
    when brothers dwell in unity!
It is like the precious oil on the head,
    running down on the beard,
on the beard of Aaron,
    running down on the collar of his robes!
It is like the dew of Hermon,
    which falls on the mountains of Zion!
For there the Lord has commanded the blessing,
    life forevermore.
—Psalm 133

# 14

# THE SECRET OF TEAMWORK

Unity is one of those topics that at first glance may seem rather simple and easily attained, but with a little life experience, and some familiarity with the history of the church as well as of political organizations and businesses, we quickly realize it is far from easy to achieve.

This psalm does not delve into all those complexities; rather, it celebrates the achievement of unity. But for us truly to appreciate what it is celebrating, and how it directs us to achieve the beauty of true unity, it is worth realizing just how difficult humans find it to follow where this psalm points.

To begin with, not all unity is thought to be, without exception, a good thing from a Christian point of view. If you know your Bible, you will know the story of the first human attempt to regain godlike unity, which was the building of a massive heavenward tower. This was judged by God to be idolatrous. Since then humans, in their frailty and fallenness, have many times attempted to achieve a human-centered form of unity. Even dictatorships give us a unity of sorts through the barbarism of those dictatorships is a wickedness that no amount of claims to unity can in the end deny.

So not all unity is good, and, in fact, even in the church sometimes there can be attempts to gain unity at the expense of higher values. We are called to be peacemakers but not to be liars in order to achieve peace. We are called to speak the truth in love so that we can all grow up into true unity, as Paul puts it in his letter to the Ephesians (4:15–16). The sort of unity that the Christian church wants is the kind that is around the truth of the gospel.

But then, having in these preliminary remarks said that not all unity is necessarily good—in fact, some unity can be wicked—we perhaps need to give a name to that form of false unity to distinguish it from true unity. There can be uniformity that is not unity, that is, an external, rigid, even forced agreement, which is very different from actual unity, which is oneness of mind and heart around the truth.

Unity, though, is not only to be distinguished from uniformity but also to be held up as a much-needed value in our society today. Historically, unity has been hard to achieve—the true kind that is unity around truth—and church history witnesses to innumerable councils that have attempted, sometimes failed, to achieve it. But while that historical witness shows us that this side of the fall, we will always find it difficult to achieve unity, unity seems to be becoming ever harder for us to experience today. We have only to look at the political sphere or the home life of many people today to realize that for some reason or other, we are finding it harder to achieve the beautiful unity that this psalm celebrates.

Why is that? Or to put it another way, what is the secret of teamwork or true unity? We are going to answer that question under three headings. Those three headings are: the pleasure of unity, the origin of unity, and then, finally, the blessing of unity.

## 1) The Pleasure of Unity

> Behold, how good and pleasant it is
> when brothers dwell in unity! (v. 1)

I am summarizing verse 1 by the title "The Pleasure of Unity," because this verse is not considering the goodness of unity from the aspect of philosophical goodness or from the study of ethics; this is not goodness in a cerebral, academic sense. The goodness that is being considered here is that unity is not only "good" but also "pleasant." This is the sort of goodness that is experientially pleasant. All goodness is pleasant, but the particular aspect of goodness being considered here is that it is pleasant. I call it "the pleasure of unity" because it is not so much saying that unity is pleasant in the sense of something mild and moderate, but in the sense of a pleasure that counters our tendency to run from unity, thinking that the fun is somewhere else.

Pleasure today can mean an experience that is morally wrong as well as one that is good. In fact, the lie is out that satisfying pleasure comes from things that are bad. But, to paraphrase C. S. Lewis, the Devil can create no pleasures of his own but can only corrupt the pleasures that God has created. So goodness considered by itself, and here specifically in relation to unity, gives pleasure.

This point about the pleasure of unity is very important for discovering the secret of teamwork, or true unity, because what often prevents people from doing the hard work that true unity always involves is the idea that the real pleasure comes from self-assertion, or grabbing what one wants, at the expense of what other people need—the sort of behavior, in short, that always makes true unity harder to achieve. Instead, this psalm is claiming right at the start that unity is a pleasurable experience and a pleasure greater than the contrasting experience of disunity, whatever pleasures we are tempted to think might be on offer down that alternative path of self. Instead, unity, which requires some compromise of our personal preferences, is a pleasure greater than the pleasure of self-seeking.

The great conductor Leonard Bernstein was once asked what was the hardest position to fill in an orchestra. He replied that the hardest position to fill was that of second fiddle. To play that part requires great skill and also a willingness to be relatively more obscure, to be second fiddle. Yet without the contribution that second fiddle and other second chairs in an orchestra provide, the sound is not harmonious.

This psalm may actually have been written to celebrate the brotherly unity that David experienced when he was crowned king and all the tribes gathered to him as one after having been divided for so long under the reign of Saul. For them to gather together as one took the humility for some to play second fiddle for the sake of the pleasure of being one together. Perhaps there is someone with whom you need to find unity. Perhaps what is stopping you is the feeling that it is not worth playing second fiddle to achieve that humility. It is worth it; there is pleasure in unity, a beautiful harmony. So, first, is the pleasure of unity.

## 2) The Origin of Unity

> It is like the precious oil on the head,
>     running down on the beard,
> on the beard of Aaron,
>     running down on the collar of his robes!
> It is like the dew of Hermon,
>     which falls on the mountains of Zion! (vv. 2–3a)

We have already hinted that unity is achieved partly through being willing to put yourself second. But the images that verse 2 and the first part of verse 3 describe show us where that desire for unity originates. It says, "It is like the precious oil on the head, running down on the beard, on the beard of Aaron, running down on the collar of his robes! It is like the dew of Hermon, which falls on the mountains of Zion!"

Having said that unity is pleasurable, these images of unity do not immediately seem pleasurable to most people today. What could be pleasurable about having oil poured down your head, so much that it goes onto your beard, so much that it drips off your beard and runs down your collar? The response of most people to that description is not nowadays, "How wonderful!" but "How messy!" "Can you imagine," the thought process of the average person today would be, "how long it would take to get all that oil out of your hair?" But before we assume that this description is simply a little disgusting, notice that the next image is more immediately appealing: "It is like the dew of Hermon, which falls on the mountains of Zion!" Early morning dew, while something that might wet your shoes, still today has a feeling of renewal and pleasure for many. Given, then, that the second of the two images appears potentially pleasant, we should carefully consider what was being communicated at the time by both of these images so we can see how it applies to us today.

The first image is referring to Aaron, Moses's brother, and his consecration as a priest, which is described in the book of Exodus. The oil was a sign of God's ordaining of Aaron as high priest. The second image refers to Mount Hermon, which was the tallest mountain in Israel at 9,100 feet, and then to Mount Zion, which is about 2,400 feet. But the key to understanding these two images is the three-times-repeated refrain, "descend, descend, descend," or "running down," "running down," and "falls on." The oil runs down from the head to the beard to the collar of the robes. The dew falls down from the heights of Mount Hermon, and also from the mountains of Zion. This unity starts high and moves down; unity has its origin high up and then descends. These two images are telling us that the origin of true unity is not in our human attempts to create unity but ultimately from God. Unity is not something we achieve; it is something that comes down to us.

I've spent a little while explaining the images here, but this point about the origin of unity is so important that I want us to consider it a little more before I illustrate it and apply it. *Unity* descends from God to us. *Uniformity* is a horizontal attempt to squeeze people into getting along together, even though they have little in common. Unity is not manufactured; it pours down from on high. Paul makes the same point when he advocates for the unity that exists between Jews and Gentiles, not by appealing to what they need to give up in order to get along together but to what they have in common as Christians. In Ephesians 1 Paul praises God for all that he has done for his people. In chapter 2 he describes what God has done as centering upon the grace of God in Christ received through faith, not by works. Then in the second half of chapter 2 Paul emphasizes that the unity in God's people is achieved through focusing on the fact that we are one in Christ. It is "in him." That is, unity descends. When Christians are not acting in a unified way, what they need to do is remember that they are one; they do not need to manufacture a horizontal uniformity but recognize anew their vertical (and therefore horizontal) unity.

When Paul makes that point in Ephesians, he is reflecting Jesus's great prayer in John 17 for his disciples toward the end of his ministry. Jesus there prayed that his disciples would be one as the Father and the Son are one. That is, our unity as Christians is not just a reflection but an *expression* of God's unity in the Trinity. Or, in other words, as this psalm beautifully portrays it, true unity *comes down*. It flows down from the head of the body, Christ, through to the rest of the body. It starts at the top of the mountain and by grace descends to the whole of the new creation in Christ.

So we have had, first, the pleasure of unity. It is good and pleasant to be united with each other as brothers and sisters. That is a motivation for us to flee things that would divide, because unity is pleasurable. Second we have the origin of unity. True unity originates in God and is achieved by Christ's work on the cross, and our experience of unity comes as we as Christians remember that we are one in him and therefore one in each other. Let me illustrate the origin of unity like this. There is a piece of doggerel that goes: "Believe as I believe, no more nor less; / That I am right and no one else, confess; / Feel as I feel, think as I think, / Look as I look, do as I do / *Then* I'll have fellowship with you."

But unity has its origin not in our personal preferences about music, or culture, or class, or race, but in Christ himself. Attempting to achieve unity without doctrinal clarity about the truth of the gospel is pointless. Diversity without unity of truth is division under another name. And unity that is attempted through cultural imitation of a human personality is verging on being cultic more than Christian. Our unity comes from the top down, from Christ down, like oil falling down, like dew coming down. It *descends*.

That emphasis on descent in this psalm is surely deliberate, because all these psalms are *ascending* psalms. It is telling us, as we come to the end of the Psalms of Ascent, that unity comes only from God. Therefore, if you wish to be one, you need first to be one with Christ through faith in him. It also means that if you are a Christian but find your unity with another believer strained, the origin of renewed unity is to renew your devotion to Christ through daily Bible reading, prayer, and abiding in Christ, that you may be one with each other as you are one in him as God himself is one in the Trinity.

So we have the pleasure of unity: seek it, for it is pleasurable. We have the origin of unity: seek it through faith in Christ from whom all true unity comes. Then, we have the blessing of unity.

### 3) The Blessing of Unity

> For there the LORD has commanded the blessing,
>     life forevermore. (v. 3b)

This is the second half of verse 3. The Hebrew word translated here as "forevermore" has the sense of life in its furthest expanse, and so can look backward or forward, and is defined by its reference. Here it is referring to what the Lord has commanded, so this is life that lasts forever. The Hebrews, no doubt, had a less developed sense of eternity than we do, since we stand this side of the resurrection of Christ. Yet the concept of eternity itself is, for us also, one that needs negative words like *endless* and *infinite* to describe it, as we are talking about an existence that is not time-bound, so beyond our experience, and defined by the eternal God.

The word at the start of this part of the verse is emphatic: "for *there* . . . ," "there" referring to what Graeme Goldsworthy termed God's people in God's place under God's rule or command. In that situation God has commanded his blessing, which is this eternal life— not simply life that goes on forever, but the blessing of ceaseless praise forever with the good God of all.

This poem of unity, then, ends with a description of the benefits of being in the community of God, his people, as one together. In that place, as we gather together in our churches, there is the command, or Word, of God that goes out, and around which we gather, and which points us to the blessing of eternal life.

The unity in the Spirit is so precious, so pleasant, that it is worth giving up our own rights, preferences, hobbyhorses, cultural ideals, benefits, stature, reputation, and honor to maintain. Paul urges us to be eager to maintain the unity of the Spirit. Unity is pleasurable. It has its origin in God himself. For us to be one shows the world that we are in Christ and that Christ is in God. Our unity is an apologetic for the Trinity of God. That unity is not uniformity and cannot be achieved at the expense of the truth of the gospel, for the origin of that unity is in Christ. But true unity in Christ in the community of his people is the location for the delivery of his Word, the blessing through which we may find life forevermore.

I want to present to you this diamond of unity, with its facets of the pleasure of unity, the origin of unity, and the blessing of unity, as something eminently desirable. Perhaps there is someone whom you have not spoken to for many years. "How good and pleasant it is when brothers dwell in unity"—would you like that unity? It is pleasant. Then seek it through finding your renewal in Christ and uniting around him rather than dividing over any differences you may have. Perhaps you have a friend or a companion with whom you are experiencing some friction. She said this, you said that, you wanted one way, she wanted the other—you couldn't have your cake, so you ate each other. If you are in Christ, then the first thing is to renew your connection to him. That is the origin of unity—to bow before Christ, submit to his Word, read the Bible, pray, and repent of your sins. Then come to the one with whom you are experiencing disunity, in a position of mutual submission before Christ, and the things with which you are in disagreement will seem so minor you may find that you are almost embarrassed to even mention them ever again.

Perhaps you have been avoiding going to church for some time because you had an experience in church in which you felt someone said something harsh to you, and your reputation was tarnished. Consider the pleasure of unity. Surely you want it, to be in the community of brothers and sisters. Consider the origin of unity. You do not have to agree with people on the color of the carpet, or the style of music, or the size of the building, or minutes of the committee meeting. Instead, you have a unity that originates in Christ. Then consider the blessing of that unity. Here is where the Word, which brings eternal life if it is combined with repentance and faith, is found. Would you give up that opportunity to be offered the Word of life because of a disagreement that happened in the past? Or will you find the pleasure, the origin, and the blessing of unity?

A Song of Ascents.
Come, bless the Lord, all you servants of the Lord,
    who stand by night in the house of the Lord!
Lift up your hands to the holy place
    and bless the Lord!
May the Lord bless you from Zion,
    he who made heaven and earth!
—Psalm 134

# 15

# THE END OF THE JOURNEY

We come now to the last psalm in the Psalms of Ascent, and as we do I hope you are immediately conscious that, for the psalmist, the end of the journey is a good place to be. Often we start out on a path, or a career, or along some trajectory of life, and as we come to the end we have a sense of disappointment that it is not as good as we had hoped it would be. Even if we win our sports league, or our team gets the crown at the end of the season, the next morning life must go on, and even the best of human journeys can end with a sense of at least mild disappointment.

But not here. This journey ends with unmitigated praise, thanksgiving, rejoicing, celebrating, and—its most prominent word repeated three times, one time for each of the verses—blessing. We will need to look very carefully at that word *blessing*, for it is the key that unlocks not only this psalm but the whole series of psalms with which we have been journeying, these Songs of Ascent; but before we specifically consider what it means to bless God, and what it means to be blessed by God, I want us to start with a simple but utterly essential realization that, whatever it means, it means something good.

When I attended Cambridge, a story was often told to undergraduates as they considered what career path to take, what journey to embark upon, about a person who arranges his life very carefully but does so without consideration of the claims of Christ. First, he plans to graduate well with a good degree, then he plans to go to the city and get a job in a bank, and then he plans to work his way up until he can buy a house in the suburbs, get married, and have children. Then he plans to take on the bank himself, as a senior director, and receive all the plaudits of the world. As the story unfolded we would ask, "And then?" or "What next?" as the journey continued. After college, a career; after the career, a family; after the family, retirement. "And then?" Golf perhaps, or a retirement home somewhere nice and pleasant. "And then?" we would ask. Enjoying their grandchildren. "And then?" we would ask. "What next?"

And as the journey continued, it became obvious that if the end of the journey is not a blessed place to be, then the whole journey itself is null and void. So I want you to notice that this passage, right at the start as we just begin to introduce its main theme now, is showing us that the end of the journey with God is a place of unmitigated goodness. There is no disappointment here, not a whiff, not a particle, not a nano-minuscule moment of disappointment. The person who follows this gospel journey on a pilgrimage with God through his life will end that journey with unmitigated, unparalleled, untarnished, complete, and utter blessing.

So as we introduce this passage, I want us to realize that it is simply telling us that a life with God ends well. Other lifestyles may accumulate more temporary plaudits and more possessions, but a life with God is one that ends well; and as Shakespeare put it, all is well that ends well. Those who win the race may not have been able to stop halfway around for a tub of ice cream, but the fact that they win the race at the end makes any suffering or difficulty on the path more than worth it. By contrast, this psalm implicitly is showing us a life that does not end like this is not a journey worth following. It is not worth living a life in which you are frightened of death or of the judgment to come, or in which you are unsure what today's activity will bring you tomorrow, as one day you face the living Lord.

The Psalm is saying instead to come on this journey, the journey of God, the journey that leaves behind the fake and the nominal Christianity to embark on a journey of radical discipleship, following Christ wherever he calls, for that journey ends well.

That is the feeling of the psalm. It is celebration! We have arrived! It is coming to the last homey house and realizing that the journey through the wilds was definitely worth it. But, of course, the question that occurs once we have made these immediate observations is, what makes it so good? What makes following the Christian path, the way of the pilgrim seeking first the kingdom of God, so good by ending so well? We come now, having introduced the theme of the psalm of ending well, to the three-time-repeated word *blessing* and the central proposition of this psalm: *a life lived for God is a life that blesses God and a life that is blessed by God.*

## 1) A Life That Blesses God

> Come, bless the LORD, all you servants of the LORD,
> who stand by night in the house of the LORD!
> Lift up your hands to the holy place
> and bless the LORD! (vv. 1–2)

"A life that blesses God" describes the first two verses of the psalm, both of which urge us to bless God. Picture the pilgrims arriving at the temple late at night. They have been journeying all day, and now they arrive and call upon those who are serving in the temple to rejoice with them. We know that the temple was never left unattended (1 Chron. 9:33), and there were always servants of the Lord tending to the temple and assuring its proper condition and readiness for the great services of the next day. The pilgrims who have just arrived call out, "Come, bless the LORD," to those who are serving in the temple, urging them not simply to go through the motions of tending to the ceremonies of the temple but to be focused upon blessing God.

To "stand . . . in the house of the LORD" was a euphemism for ministering in the temple, for the priests stood as they administered the sacrifices. It was common to lift up hands in prayer and praise, and so both pilgrims and priests are urged to raise their hands and bless the Lord. In the New Testament all Christians are priests, for we have access to God through the Great High Priest Jesus Christ, and so we are to urge each other to serve in God's house, and for God's purposes, with a focus upon blessing God and not just going through the motions.

Before we illustrate and then apply this point—that a life lived for God blesses God and ends well and therefore is to be pursued—we need to be clear what it really means to bless God. How can we humans bless

God? How can an inferior person, a subject, bless a superior person, a king? How can a created person, a human, bless his or her creator, the God of heaven and earth? Scholars have attempted various solutions to this conundrum, because the idea of our being able to bless God does not merely occur in this psalm but is fairly frequent throughout the Old Testament. Psalm 72:18 says, "Blessed be the LORD, the God of Israel"; and Genesis 24:27 says, "Blessed be the LORD, the God of my master Abraham, who has not forsaken his steadfast love and his faithfulness toward my master." How can this be? How can it be true not only that "blessed be Abram by God Most High" (Gen. 14:19), but also "blessed be God Most High" (Gen. 14:20)? Or how can we not only receive blessing from God but actually give blessing to God?

Perhaps we need to ask another question: what does it actually mean to be blessed? In English the word *bless* means to pronounce that something is good or to confer goodness upon something in a religious sense, and the word may have its origins in the Old English word *blood*. A benediction, frequently used as a synonym, means "a good saying," coming from the Latin root meaning to say that something is good or well. The Hebrew word used here for "blessed" may have the root of meaning to kneel before something or someone, though not all agree with that derivation.

Perhaps it is simplest to say, by analogy, that this word *blessed*, often used of us blessing God and of God blessing us, functions similarly to when we say that we speak to God and that God speaks to us. When we speak to God, we are speaking, and we speak human words necessarily. When we bless God, we are blessing and give human blessing necessarily. When God speaks, he speaks God's words, and when he blesses, he gives God's blessings. So the blessing of God by humans is a human declaration that God is good. What the pilgrims here are urging the priests to do ("Come, bless the LORD") and what they themselves will do ("lift up your hands to the holy place and bless the LORD!") is to live a life, to utter words and do deeds, in such a way that makes clear that God is good. They are being urged to live a life that honors God, to live a life that focuses upon God, to live for God. They are being urged to say that God is good, that he is blessed. They are not adding to the divine, eternal, complete, sufficient blessedness of God in his own person; they are witnessing to it. They are declaring, in their own experience, through their journey, that they have witnessed that a life lived for God is the happiest kind of life. They are blessing God that he is blessed and worth living for. It is their witness, their declaration.

Now I am going to illustrate and apply this point about us blessing God, but there is one final aspect of this that, very briefly, we need to clarify, and that is whether the hands lifted up in praise to God are mandatory, exemplary, or specific to this context here. It is fairly clear in the Old Testament that different body positions were used in worship—kneeling; falling flat on the face; even dancing, in the case of King David; standing; lifting up hands; bowing the head; taking off shoes—to indicate reverence and awe and joy toward God. This is not because a certain body position, hands raised high or low, is necessary or that one of them is preferred over the others. It is, rather, that when we realize how blessed is God, being ourselves psychosomatic units—that is, people who are not only souls but bodies, and whose feelings influence their body positions—when we truly and honestly bless God, and say, "You're worth it," this will no doubt influence what we today call our "body language."

When someone scores a touchdown, fans pump the air; here the pilgrims are lifting up their hands. People are free to indicate their excitement in other ways or their commitment in other forms—standing or kneeling or sitting with concentration; leaning forward in their seats; or raising hands—as long as it is not distracting to others, for that could defeat the purpose of honoring God by inadvertently drawing attention to yourself. There is, of course, a difference between private worship and congregational public worship in this regard, public worship requiring more sensitivity to the tastes and presence of people of different personal dispositions.

Now, let me illustrate what it means to live a life that blesses God like this. When the Bible commentator Matthew Henry came to the end of his life, he is said to have blessed God in this way: "Would you like to know where I am? I am at home in my Father's house, in the mansion prepared for me. I am where I want to be. My sowing time is done, and

I am reaping. My joy is the joy of the harvest. Would you like to know how it is with me? I am made perfect in holiness. Grace is swallowed up in victory. Would you like to know what I am doing? I see God, not as through a glass darkly, but face-to-face. I am engaged in the sweet enjoyment of my precious Redeemer. Would you like to know what blessed company I keep? It is better than the best on earth. Here are the holy angels and the spirits of just men made perfect. I am with many of my former acquaintances with whom I worked and prayed, and who have come here before me. Lastly, would you like to know how long this will continue? It is a dawn that never fades. After millions and millions of ages it will be as fresh as it is now. Therefore, weep not for me! Amen!"[1]

Therefore, as we consider such a life that ends well, the application of this point about life that ends in blessing God is obvious: live that way too; follow this journey on your pilgrimage to God. But finally, not only is this a life that blesses God, and therefore shows us how wonderful it is to live like that, it is also a life that ends in being blessed by God.

## 2) A Life That Ends in Being Blessed by God

> May the LORD bless you from Zion,
> he who made heaven and earth! (v. 3)

Verse 3 carries on that frequent theme in the Bible, that those who live to bless God are blessed by God. So the very Creator of the whole universe in all its magisterial scope blesses us. A life that is blessed by God is to be sought more than anything else. Material possessions, power, fame, and worldly success can be found while ignoring God. But such lives, I am afraid to say, are more warnings to avoid than examples to follow. History is littered with examples of men who have built their mansions and shriveled away in tiny rooms in those mansions, gradually estranged from family, friends, and at the end even themselves. Charles IX, who ordered the Saint Bartholomew's Day massacres, said at the end of his journey, "What blood! What murders! I know not where I am. How will all this end? What shall I do? I am lost forever. I know it."

---

[1] *Our Daily Bread*, Sunday, May 27, 2004.

But a life that is blessed by God is a life that is worth living and pursuing and going on that journey together with all our passion and energy and time and commitment—everything we can muster—for we can see that it ends with God's blessing as the journey is completed. The blessing here is the beginning of the famous priestly blessing from Numbers 6:

> The LORD bless you and keep you;
> the LORD make his face to shine upon you and be gracious to you;
> the LORD lift up his countenance upon you and give you peace.
>     (vv. 24–26)

To be blessed by God means to be in the covenant of God of the people of God and a recipient of the favor of God. God's blessing is his salvation, his presence, his help, his love—ultimately God himself. The blessing of God is that God blesses you in that you have God, the maker of heaven and earth, and that he is for you, not against you. God's blessing is God and enjoyment of him.

How can we humans receive such a blessing? Do we receive it because we bless God, or because we live morally upright lives and try to do what is right? Throughout the Old Testament the blessing of God was sought through the prescribed sacrifice of animals yet with an awareness that more was needed than a wooly sheep or a goat to atone for sins. So we come to the New Testament, to Christ, and to his perfect blessing pronounced to the thief at his side who had no time to do anything of merit to earn that blessing but simply believed: "Today you will be with me in Paradise" (Luke 23:43).

That blessing of God is the end of the journey that every sensible person desires. To receive it means to put our faith in that same Jesus who died on the cross for our sins so that we might receive his righteousness. That blessing from him, despite our many failures and foibles, comes with great joy, pure grace, and unmerited favor—just like that thief on the cross—when we say, "Remember me when you come into your kingdom" (Luke 23:42).

And so the journey ends through the prism of these Psalms of Ascent. They start low, leaving on their journey with trepidation; and they end high, with unembarrassed, unashamed, untarnished blessing and praise with a finale that has no disappointment to it whatsoever. It is purely and simply blessing to God and blessing to us. It comes to us through the agency of the covenant of God, his blessing to Abraham, through David, and at the cross and Christ's resurrection from the dead—the gospel that is now preached to the ends of the earth.

And as we come to the end of this particular journey, I wish to point you toward this finishing point. Is this where your life is going? Will you complete your life like Samuel Rutherford, who said, "O, that all my brethren did know what a master I have served, and what peace I have this day! I shall sleep in Christ, and when I awake shall be satisfied with his likeness"; like Richard Baxter, who said, "I bless God I have a well-grounded assurance of my eternal happiness, and great peace and comfort within," and when asked right before the end how he was doing, replied, "Almost well."

Is that how our story will end? Is that the journey we are on, that is, a pilgrimage with Christ for our companion, with heaven for our goal, with the blessing of God on our lips, and the assurance of God's blessing in our lives? If it is, rejoice with no disappointment. You have chosen the path less traveled that ends well, and all's well that ends well. And if that is not the path you are on, then without delay begin the journey that ends like this.

# GENERAL INDEX

# SCRIPTURE INDEX

179

Josh Moody and a team of internationally renowned Edwards scholars ask the question:

# What did Jonathan Edwards Believe about Justification?

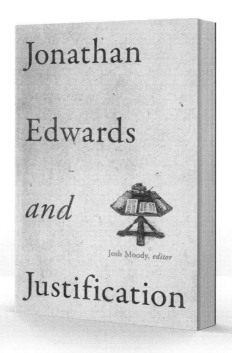

"Provides insight and guidance not only for understanding the thought of Jonathan Edwards in his historical context, but also for wrestling with the current debate regarding the doctrine of justification by faith."
**DAVID S. DOCKERY,** President, Union University

"This volume considers Edwards responsibly and correctly. A balanced assessment of Edwards as an orthodox thinker, yet one with 'creativity, spice, and derring-do.'"
**KENNETH P. MINKEMA,** Executive Editor and Director, Jonathan Edwards Center at Yale University

"A significant work that advances the growing scholarship on Jonathan Edwards and contributes to the current debates on justification."
**DENNIS P. HOLLINGER,** President and the Colman M. Mockler Distinguished Professor of Christian Ethics, Gordon-Conwell Theological Seminary

# The True Gospel as Revealed in the Book of Galatians

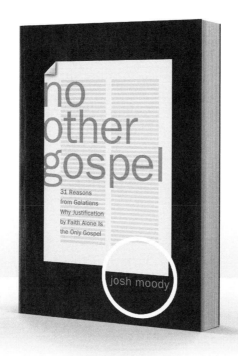

"These expositions are clear, well-organized, exegetically careful, and theologically faithful. These qualities make for very good preaching and a very good book."

**KEVIN DEYOUNG,** Senior Pastor, University Reformed Church, East Lansing, MI

"Paul's Letter to the Galatians so strongly and passionately articulates the gospel of grace that it has proved transforming in many generations of preachers from Luther to Wesley and beyond. Here Moody reinforces that heritage for the twenty-first century."

**D. A. CARSON,** Research Professor of New Testament, Trinity Evangelical Divinity School

"Blends attention to the text, theological insight, and pastoral application in a model of scriptural exposition. His focus on Galatians is a great choice, since this letter addresses so clearly the nature and importance of the gospel."

**DOUGLAS J. MOO,** Blanchard Professor of New Testament, Wheaton College